Federalism in the Forest

American Governance and Public Policy series
Series Editor: Barry Rabe, University of Michigan

Federalism in the Forest

National versus State Natural Resource Policy

Tomas M. Koontz

Georgetown University Press / Washington, D.C.

Georgetown University Press, Washington, D.C.
© 2002 by Georgetown University Press. All rights reserved.
Printed in the United States of America

10 9 8 7 6 5 4 3 2 1   2002

This volume is printed on acid-free offset book paper.

Library of Congress Cataloging-in-Publication Data

Koontz, Tomas M.
   Federalism in the forest : national versus state natural resource policy /
Tomas M. Koontz.
       p.   cm. — (American Governance and Public Policy Series)
   Includes bibliographical references (p.).
   ISBN 0-87840-374-4 (pbk.)
   1. Forest Policy—United States.   2. Administrative agencies—United
States—Management.   3. Government productivity—United States.   I. Title.
II. Series.

SD565 .K66 2002
333.75′0973—dc21
                                                                    2002190230

For Kristin, Amelia, and Rosemary—
the lights of my life

Contents

Tables and Figures

Preface

Indiana University at Bloomington is blessed with an enviable location. With abundant forested hills within a half-hour drive, the campus is well-situated within a state that otherwise is known for its flat farmland. Indiana University also is blessed with the Workshop in Political Theory and Policy Analysis. This center of scholarship provides a home for interdisciplinary work among political scientists, economists, ecologists, sociologists, anthropologists, and other scholars from around the world.

It is through a combination of these two assets that I first became interested in forest policy issues. I learned that the forests of southern Indiana were owned and managed by a variety of private and public parties, including individuals, corporations, nonprofit organizations, state government agencies, and national government agencies. At the same time, Elinor Ostrom and others at the Workshop were developing the International Forestry Resources and Institutions (IFRI) research program, with the purpose of examining physical and social factors affecting community organization and forest management around the world. Through my association with the IFRI program, I became increasingly interested in questions about forest policy in our own "backyard," especially in differences between types of public jurisdiction. Thus began my work leading to this book.

In the pages that follow, I offer detailed comparisons of state and federal public forest management. I use these comparisons to describe and explain policy performance in a federal system. Although in one sense the book is about forest policy, in a broader sense it is about federalism, devolution, citizen participation, and agency policymaking.

My aim is to provide rigorous empirical research, linked to theory, that is nevertheless accessible to readers without expertise in forestry or policy analysis. My hope is that scholars and students at the advanced undergraduate and graduate levels, as well as other readers interested in public policy and natural resources, will find food for thought in the ideas I present.

Acknowledgments

I owe debts of gratitude to many people who helped me complete this project. Elinor Ostrom provided invaluable guidance throughout my graduate work, and she played a crucial role in my doctoral journey and intellectual growth at Indiana University. Rosemary O'Leary contributed important feedback, particularly during the design stage of this research. I also am appreciative of assistance from Ken Bickers, Kerry Krutilla, and Leroy Rieselbach. Helpful comments on portions of this project were provided by Yu-che Chen, Charlie Schweik, and Paul Turner, as well as colleagues to whom I presented my work at meetings of the Western Political Science Association and the Midwestern Political Science Association.

During the course of my field research, I called on the generosity of family and friends while conducting interviews in several locations in each of four states. In Ohio, I am especially thankful to Steve Davis; in Washington I appreciated the generosity of Gael Owen, Nathan and Andrea Harrison, and Eric and Kirsten Barkman; in Oregon I enjoyed an extended stay with Linda and Tom Davis and the hospitality of Chuck and Flerida Lund. I also benefited from Fred Thompson, who provided office space and a presentation opportunity at the Atkinson Graduate School of Management at Willamette University.

I would not have gained such extensive information for this book without the cooperation of nearly 100 forest agency officials, who took the time to answer many questions and provide numerous documents—sometimes after extensive research. These public servants were always helpful and accommodating in discussing a wide range of topics. I also gained important insights from conversations with more than five dozen citizens who were interested in forest management issues and spoke openly about their experiences and views.

I appreciate the financial assistance provided by the Workshop in Political Theory and Policy Analysis at Indiana University, National Science Foundation Grant SBR 9521918, Indiana University Graduate School, and the Center for the Study of Institutions, Population, and Environmental Change at Indiana University.

The journey from dissertation research to completed book was helped by the guiding hands and encouragement of Gail Grella at Georgetown University Press and series editor Barry Rabe, along with constructive feedback from three anonymous reviewers.

Although the pursuit of knowledge is important, there are, of course, things that are even more valuable. I am thankful for the love and support of my family, especially my wife Kristin.

Abbreviations

APA	Administrative Procedure Act
BMP	best management practice
FACA	Federal Advisory Committee Act
FPA	Forest Practices Act
HCP	Habitat Conservation Plan
K-V Act	Knutsen-Vandenberg Act
MUSYA	Multiple-Use, Sustained-Yield Act
NEPA	National Environmental Policy Act
NFMA	National Forest Management Act
OMB	Office of Management and Budget
ORV	off-road vehicle
SEPA	State Environmental Policy Act
TSI	timber stand improvement

Part One

Agency Policy Performance in a Federal System

1 Does Devolution Matter?

On March 15, 1996, Charles Oliver, an employee of the U.S. Department of Agriculture (USDA) Forest Service, was literally beaten and thrown out of a ranchers' meeting in eastern Arizona. After refusing to leave the meeting, which was held in a public school, Oliver was "attacked, hit on the back of the head and neck, kicked, pulled by the ear, wrenched by the shoulder, and finally, picked up and thrown into the schoolyard" (Yozwiak 1996). Oliver subsequently named three ranchers in a federal lawsuit. One of the alleged attackers, sixty-five-year-old rancher John Joy, remarked that federal government restrictions were forcing ranchers and loggers out of the public forests in the region.

Joy was not alone in his displeasure with federal land management. County officials in nearby Nye County, Nevada, passed a resolution declaring that federal lands in the county belong to the state of Nevada. In attempting to assert this resolution, County Commissioner Dick Carver drove a county bulldozer past an armed Forest Service agent and onto the Toiyabe National Forest, as a crowd of 200 people—many of them armed—cheered him on. Carver's 1994 trespass led to litigation and a spot on the cover of *Time* magazine as a symbol for increasing hostility over federal land ownership in the West. Such hostility also is evident in the pipe bombs found in New Mexico's Gila Wilderness, gunshots fired at a Forest Service biologist in California, and a bomb that destroyed a Forest Service ranger's van parked in his Nevada driveway (Larson 1995).

In the legal arena, activists have circulated petitions to urge Idaho's governor to declare state ownership of the more than 33 million acres of federal land in the state (Rauber 1995). Representative Jim Bunn proposed a bill in Congress calling for the transfer of 2.5 million acres of timber-rich federal land to the state of Oregon—a move supported by counties in which the land is located (*Register-Guard* 1996).

Similarly, Representative Jim Hansen called for a bill to transfer control of certain federal land to the state of Utah (Rauber 1995). Senator Larry Craig of Idaho, who chaired the Senate Republican Policy Committee, vowed to introduce a new National Forest Management Act that would allow the Forest Service to contract out forest management to state governments (Margolis 1997). Craig subsequently championed a bill allowing states or nonprofit groups to manage certain national forests (*Idaho Statesman* 1998). More recently, many western states have begun planning to create endangered species offices and to press the federal government to devolve endangered species authority to states (Stuebner 2001).

Of course, conflict over the role of the federal government is not a new phenomenon. The question of appropriate jurisdictions for various government activities is a fundamental issue in American politics. Periodically, much debate centers on initiatives to transfer a variety of social programs from the federal level to the local or state level. For example, Richard Nixon's "New Federalism" aimed to provide local government with more freedom to carry out programs. In his first term, Ronald Reagan pursued consolidations of block grants to transfer authority (and less funding) to the states. He also proposed turning over two welfare programs—Aid to Families with Dependent Children (AFDC) and food stamps—to the states. With Newt Gingrich at the helm, the 104th Congress generated proposals to devolve several federal social programs to the state level. Even Democrats got into the act, as Bill Clinton in 1996 signed into law a welfare reform bill granting increased responsibility and authority to state governments. During these debates over the appropriate levels of government responsibility, proponents of state primacy claim that states would provide more effective and efficient administration; opponents counter that this devolution would thwart the achievement of certain policy goals.

In the realm of natural resource policy, debates often focus on questions of private versus public control. For example, the "Sagebrush Rebellion" in the late 1970s and early 1980s spawned calls for the wholesale privatization of federal lands in the West. In 1982 Secretary of the Interior James Watt fueled controversy with a plan to sell 35 million acres of federal land to private owners. Scholars have joined the privatization debate, examining questions about public versus private control of natural resources. John Baden and Richard Stroup (1981), for example, have long championed the "new resource economics" school of thought, suggesting that privatization is economically and environmentally superior to public control. On the other hand, Kai Lee (1993) and others emphasize the importance of public management to provide better stewardship of natural resources.

Although the difference between public and private ownership is generally understood, many citizens do not readily distinguish between federal and state public lands. Nevertheless, choices among governmental jurisdictions lie at the very core of federalism. This is no less true in public lands management than in education, health care, welfare, gun control, transportation, or any number of other policy sectors. Yet the subject of intergovernmental differences is a largely neglected area within natural resource policy inquiry. We need to delve more deeply within public management, asking hard questions about policymaking in federal, state, and local contexts. That is, for natural resource decisions that are made in the public arena, what processes and outcomes are likely to occur at different levels of government? Are there systematic differences between higher and lowers levels in terms of policy performance, and if so, why? In other words, from a policy perspective, does devolution matter?

In this work I tackle these questions about natural resource policy in a federal system. Because many of the policies affecting this country's natural resources are created and implemented by government agencies, my focus is on agency policymaking. In particular, I compare and contrast public forests in the jurisdiction of the federal government (the national forests, managed by the USDA Forest Service) with public forests in the jurisdiction of state governments (state forests, managed by state forestry departments). I address these questions with theoretical arguments that are based primarily in political science and public administration theory, as well as insights from economics, organizational theory, and forestry.

Which Level of Government Is Better?

The question of whether different governmental levels are associated with fundamentally different natural resource policies has not been widely explored. Of course, scholars have devoted ample ink to the study of higher versus lower levels of government activity, but such studies generally have not included close examination of natural resource policy. Instead, they have focused on other governmental functions, such as taxation, wealth redistribution, economic stabilization, and public service provision. Advocates of greater local control have praised the merits of lower-level government jurisdiction, whereas skeptics have cited the importance of federal-level authority.

Some scholars stress the benefits of policymaking by lower-level governments in a federal system. They typically emphasize the advantages in terms of three key elements: citizen involvement, responsiveness, and cost efficiency. First, the existence of a diverse array of local governments promotes citizen involvement in self-governance; individuals are less likely to fall into the "central government trap" of waiting for distant officials to solve problems for them (Ostrom 1987). The very roots of our nation's history are firmly planted in local governance, with New England town hall meetings and Thomas Jefferson's vision of an American democracy based on citizens who actively participate in local governance because they can shape it directly.

Second, lower levels of government are expected to be more responsive to local citizens and better suited to understand local needs and preferences. Moreover, responsiveness is assured by citizens' ability to "vote with their feet"—moving to jurisdictions that provide their preferred mix of services and taxes (Tiebout 1956).

Third, lower levels of government are likely to be more cost-effective than higher levels. For services such as trash collection, police protection, and road maintenance, having multiple local governments nearby encourages citizens to compare costs with neighboring jurisdictions and demand more efficient government (Ostrom, Tiebout, and Warren 1961). Furthermore, devolution of responsibility to lower levels can lead to better matching of who pays with who benefits. This matching increases economic efficiency by reducing the tendency of citizens to demand higher levels of services for which they don't have to pay (Nelson 1995).

Skeptics of local government have supported a broader role for federal government. There are certain functions, they argue, that lower levels of government simply are not equipped to perform well. Issues that go beyond local boundaries include stabilizing the economy, accounting for externalities such as air and water pollution that cross jurisdictions, and enhancing equity (Anton 1989). In addition, the phenomenon of "voting with your feet" at the local level, which can make government more responsive, also can hinder the ability of government policy to redistribute wealth to the neediest people because wealthier people might easily relocate to protect their wealth from being redistributed (Derthick 1971). This means that government programs that are aimed at helping the underprivileged are not likely to be as successful if they are created by lower levels of government.

Differences in Policy Performance

Beyond broad-brush generalizations about which government level is "better," we can fine-tune the discussion by focusing on differences in policy performance. If we are seeking to identify "better" policy performance, it is important to distinguish between policy outputs (ends) and the process (means) of policymaking.

Policy outputs refer to decisions that have been reached. For example, if government officials are considering a proposal to zone a parcel of land as either a wilderness area or a commercial development area, their decision is a policy output. The output can be measured in terms of what land use it promotes (in this example, either ecological/aesthetic use or economic development). It also can be measured in terms of fiscal results, such as the amount of revenue it causes to be added to the tax base.

The process of policymaking is an important consideration in a democratic society. Presumably, not only do we desire the end results of a policy to be beneficial, we also care about the means by which policy decisions are made. In particular, the ability of citizens to provide input into policy decisions that affect them is an important measure of policy performance. To continue with the foregoing zoning example, regardless of whether the parcel is designated as wilderness or commercial development, the policy performance can be measured in terms of the level of citizen participation in the process of arriving at the designation.

Policy Outputs and the Functional Theory of Federalism

I turn now to the first measure of policy performance: policy outputs. In explaining policy outputs in a federal system, the "functional theory of federalism" predicts that lower and higher levels of government tend to produce different outputs (Peterson 1995). The functional theory of federalism distinguishes between two fundamentally distinct types of policy outputs: "developmental" and "redistributive." *Developmental* refers to economic development, or policy outputs that encourage economic growth in a jurisdiction. Redistributive policy outputs, on the other hand, transfer money from one set of individuals or organizations to another. Typically, *redistribution* refers to money transferred away from wealthier parties and toward poorer parties.

According to the functional theory of federalism, elected officials in lower levels of government favor developmental policies over redistributive ones. Developmental policies enhance the economic position of the government by generating business and employee taxes. In contrast, redistributive policies encourage wealthier individuals and firms—who don't want their wealth to be redistributed—to move away, which hurts the local tax base. Therefore there is little support for redistributive policies at lower levels of government, and elected officials pursuing such policies are defeated at the polls.[1]

Elected officials at higher levels of government, on the other hand, are more apt to pursue redistributive policies, which do not enhance economic development. They can do this because it is more difficult to move to another country than it is to move across state or county lines. The flight of wealth is less imminent if federal officials produce redistributive policies, and voters are less likely to punish them at the polls.

The functional theory fits well with the "voting with your feet" idea, and it has been supported with evidence from a variety of sources. Across a wide range of federal programs implemented at the local level, researchers have found that city government officials are more willing to pursue policies that help them fiscally, as opposed to those that redistribute wealth (Peterson, Rabe, and Wong 1986). For example, in a study of local housing expenditures from city and federal funds, Goetz (1995) reports that federal funds are targeted to tenant assistance for low-income households, whereas city funds are targeted to middle-income households seeking home-buying assistance. Moreover, the "devolution revolution" under President Reagan, which sought to move authority for many programs from the federal level down to state and local levels of government, was based largely on the belief that devolution would lead to fewer restrictions on economic development (Rich and White 1996).

The functional theory, as described above, applies to policy outputs from elected officials. At the state and local levels of government, voters punish elected officials who produce policies that redistribute wealth rather than grow the local economy: They vote them out of office. A limitation of the functional theory, however, is that although it can help to explain policy outputs from elected officials, many of the important public policy decisions today are made by civil servants in government agencies. In this realm the electoral mechanism is of little help in explaining policymaking because bureaucrats typically acquire their positions through merit rather than elections. Thus it is unclear whether the differences between higher and lower levels of government that are evident in policymaking by elected officials also hold true for policymaking by agency officials. For agency policymaking, the question again is: Does devolution matter?

State versus Federal Natural Resource Policy Outputs

In natural resource policy, some observers have described substantial differences between state and federal policy outputs. In particular, state and local governments are perceived as encouraging industrial activities that favor economic development over environmental protection. In competition with each other for industry, state and local governments may set less-stringent environmental standards than does the federal government in hopes of attracting business (Moe 1989). Several research studies have noted this "race to the bottom." For example, in examining environmental policy across states, Lowry (1992) finds that states competing with each other for mobile capital are not likely to regulate stationary source pollution strictly. With state and local governments jockeying for position to attract industry, it is no wonder that environmentalists often press for environmental restrictions to be determined at the federal level (Gibbins 1994).

Despite a perceived state emphasis on development for economic returns, some researchers have argued that state agencies protect natural resources and environmental quality better than do federal agencies. For example, an analysis of forest protection in Montana suggested that the state agency did a better job of protecting land from adverse impacts of timber harvesting than did the federal agency (Leal 1995). Across many of the western states, Souder and Fairfax (1996) argue that policymakers with a constitutional mandate to manage lands "in trust" successfully protect natural resources to meet their requirement to manage the productive capacity of the land in perpetuity. In addition, during the 1980s era of devolution, several states initiated successful environmental protection experiments, and in some instances states exceeded federal standards for environmental protection (Kritz 1989).

Overall, then, some disagreement remains over the question of natural resource policy outputs in a federal system. Regarding environmental protection, some researchers argue that the federal level of government produces outputs that are more protective than does the state or local level. This position is in line with the functional theory of federalism, which suggests that where environmental protection reduces economic development, we should see federal level policies performing better on environmental protection outputs. Some researchers, however, describe state governments as capable of exceeding the federal government on environmental protection outputs.

Regarding fiscal outputs in natural resource policy, lower levels of government are expected to be more cost-effective. In public land management, as Nelson (1995) explains, economic efficiency is greater at lower levels of government because costs and benefits are more closely matched. In contrast, he argues, federal public lands are managed with greater fiscal waste because those who do not pay the costs lobby for greater expenditures. The U.S. Forest Service has been a popular whipping post for those concerned about fiscal waste; several researchers have pointed to below-cost timber sales as an example of economic inefficiency (Leal 1995; O'Toole 1993; Rice 1989). As the term implies, below-cost timber sales mean that the cost to prepare, sell, and monitor timber sales on national forests exceeds the revenues generated from such sales. According to the Forest Service, the annual net loss on timber sales is about $15 million nationwide (Warrick 1997).

The Process of Policymaking

In addition to policy outputs, another measure of policy performance is the policymaking process itself. A key component of the process is the degree to which citizens are able to participate in creating policy. Citizen participation is expected to differ across levels of government in a federal system, in two fundamental ways. First, citizens favoring economic benefits may be more active and influential at lower levels. Parties seeking economic benefits tend to advocate policy devolution to lower levels of governance, where they will find regulators more attuned to promoting economic development (Sabatier 1974). Second, citizens pursuing noneconomic interests are expected to be more active at higher levels of governance (Peterson 1981, 1995; Heclo 1978). If this is true, these citizens also might wield more influence at higher levels. In fact, groups favoring noneconomic interests such as environmental preservation have grown dramatically at the federal level, increasingly focusing on federal policies (Walker 1983; Schlozman and Tierney 1983; Nash 1982; Robinson 1975).

These differences in participation patterns can be linked to the functional theory of federalism. With greater capital mobility across states than nations, elected officials at lower levels of government fear the repercussions (e.g., job losses, reduced tax base, and so forth, which can lead to unsuccessful election campaigns) from capital flight if they fail to pursue economic development. Thus, they are more likely to be open to, and encourage, participation by citizens with economic interests. Of course, the functional theory of federalism applies only to elected officials, so the reasons for any differences in citizen participation in agency policymaking remain an open, yet important, question.

Comparing State and Federal Public Forest Policy

To compare policy performance across levels of government, I analyze public forest policy in the United States. Specifically, in this book I focus on management of state and national forests in two different regions of the United States: the Midwest and the Pacific Northwest. Within each of these regions, I compare pairs of public forests located near each other sharing similar physical characteristics but with differences in governmental jurisdiction (one state, the other national).

My focus is on the role of agency decision makers in forest management policy. Although the role of elected representatives certainly is important, my emphasis on agency policymaking reflects the recognition that forest policy—indeed, any kind of public policy—is more than the enactment of laws by legislatures; agency officials are important policymakers as they implement, interpret, and "fill in the details" of broader legislative directives. As the authors of one leading environmental policy text define it, "Public policy is a course of governmental action or inaction in response to social problems" that includes choices made by political leaders, courts, and administrative agencies (Vig and Kraft 2000: 4).

Two fundamental questions guide my analysis:

1. Do state and federal agency public forest policy performances differ systematically?
2. If so, why are there such differences?

By comparing performances across levels of government in the same policy sector, during the same time period, we can discover whether there are distinct differences between higher and lower levels of agency policymaking. Then, if there are any such differences, answering the second question can explain what causes them.

It is important to note that this book diverges from traditional studies of federalism in two important ways. First, it does not emphasize the interrelations among different government jurisdictions. Although these interactions are important—and a mainstay of intergovernmental relations literature—this book instead takes a comparative approach to examine whether and why there are systematic differences between policy performance by agencies at different levels in a federal system. This approach allows better illumination of devolution and what it might bring. Second, the book does not emphasize the legal history or implications of shared power in a federal system—a task I leave to legal scholars. Instead, the focus is on the policy implications of choices about where to vest authority in a federal system.

Two Theories about Agency Policy Performance in a Federal System

Although forest policy is the specific sector I examine in this book, the theories that inform the analysis apply more generally to policymaking in a federal system. Fundamentally, two theories provide a starting point for explaining agency policy performance at higher versus lower levels of government: the functional theory of federalism and bureaucratic behavior theory.

Functional Theory of Federalism

Forest policy is well suited to application of the functional theory of federalism. Recall that the functional theory addresses policy choices between economic and noneconomic goals. Public forests increasingly have come to be valued for a wide variety of often conflicting benefits (see Hoberg 1997); two of the most prominent are timber (primarily for economic benefits) and environmental protection (primarily for noneconomic benefits). Thus, the functional theory of federalism predicts that policy made by elected officials at the state level favors timber provision more than does policy made by elected officials at the federal level. In contrast, policy made by elected officials at the federal level is expected to favor environmental protection more than does policy made by elected officials at the state level.

Bureaucratic Behavior Theory

Because agency officials are not elected, the functional theory cannot directly account for agency policy choices. Therefore we must seek theoretical insights from another area of scholarship: bureaucratic behavior. Students of bureaucratic behavior have theorized, and

empirically supported, the importance of several factors that affect
agency decision making, including rules, citizen pressure, agency officials' beliefs, and agency community.

Rules

Rules are authoritative statements that direct people to behave in certain ways. By establishing outcomes associated with particular actions,
rules provide constraints and incentives to shape action (Ostrom
1990). Rules affecting bureaucratic behavior may be initiated by
elected officials or by agency officials. The functional theory of federalism can be extended to agency policymaking through the former
source of rules. According to the functional theory, federal elected officials (the president and Congress) are more likely to create rules that
encourage federal agency personnel (in the Forest Service) to pursue noneconomic benefits such as environmental protection, whereas
state elected officials (governors and legislators) are more likely to create rules that encourage state agency personnel (in state departments
of forestry) to pursue economic benefits such as timber provision. As
long as such rules are significant determinants of agency policymaking, the functional theory of federalism should apply to agencies.

In public forest policy, elected officials may influence bureaucrats
by creating several types of rules, including laws, forest planning requirements, and budget incentives. Laws are statutory requirements
that agency officials must follow in creating and implementing policy. At the federal level, environmental laws have become increasingly
specific over the past three decades, greatly affecting agency policymaking (Hoberg 1997). For example, the National Forest Management Act created forest practice requirements that substantially reduced federal agency officials' ability to provide timber. Another type
of rule is forest plans, which are created by agencies to direct
management activities. Elected officials may enact planning requirements that determine who participates in creating plans and what the
plans must contain. In a classic study of the USDA Forest Service,
Kaufman (1960) noted that agency plans are an important means to
guide forester activities. Finally, budget incentives can significantly affect bureaucratic behavior as agency officials seek to maximize, or at

least to stabilize, their resources. In public forest policy, several critiques have emphasized the perverse budget incentives relating to timber revenues (such as the Knutsen-Vandenberg Act) that are thought to affect bureaucratic behavior at the federal level (see Budiansky 1991).

Such scholarship on the importance of rules in agency policymaking can be integrated with theories about levels of government to inform the analysis in this book. Based on the functional theory of federalism, I expect that laws, forest planning requirements, and budget incentives encourage state agency officials to pursue timber more than federal agency officials. I also anticipate that rules encourage federal officials to pursue environmental protection more than state agency officials.

Citizen Pressure

Besides rules, bureaucratic behavior theory suggests the importance of citizen pressure in affecting agency policy. By their very nature, public agencies exist to serve society, and responding to citizen demands has been a persistent element of efforts to enhance agency performance. In public forest policy, Hoberg (1997) describes the critical importance of citizens in Forest Service policymaking. Since the 1970s, he argues, citizens favoring environmental protection have used appeals and lawsuits effectively to block timber sales and protect rare species on national forests. Citizen influence in shifting policy toward greater environmental protection stemmed from the national nature of the national forests, which are "owned" by all U.S. citizens, many living far from the forests. Greater distance from forests is linked to stronger interest in environmental preservation.

In contrast, people living near public forests tend to support using them for economic benefits. Thus, state forest agency personnel are likely to face less citizen pressure to preserve forests. In other words, citizens favoring economic benefits may be more influential at lower levels of government (Peterson 1995).

Thus, I expect that in public forest policy, citizens favoring timber (who live closer to the forests) are more influential in state forest agency policymaking, whereas those favoring environmental protection (who live further from the forests) wield more influence in U.S. Forest Service policymaking.

Agency Officials' Beliefs

The third factor that bureaucratic behavior theory highlights as affecting agency policymaking is agency officials' beliefs. Agencies are composed of numerous individuals, each with views about appropriate administrative behavior and decision making. Research suggests that these beliefs are important determinants of bureaucratic decisions, especially in agencies whose members belong to cohesive professions, such as foresters, engineers, bomber pilots, carrier admirals, or attorneys (Kaufman 1960; Bendor, Taylor, and Van Gaalen 1987; Halperin 1974; Eisner and Meier 1990). In the context of federalism, little is known about whether, or how, agencies at different levels of government might attract or encourage systematically different sets of beliefs among agency members.

Agency Community

The fourth factor in bureaucratic behavior theory is agency community. Socially constructed understanding among members of an organization can powerfully influence their behavior (Ott 1989; Shafritz and Russell 1997). An important community attribute is the set of shared norms among members (Ostrom, Gardner, and Walker 1994). A public agency can encourage shared norms, as well as esprit de corps, through a variety of mechanisms, including geographic relocation and promotion from within (Kaufman 1960). These mechanisms have been applied effectively in the USDA Forest Service, as noted by Kaufman and others. Little is known, however, about agency community attributes at the state level.

Findings and Plan for the Book

My analysis reveals that there are indeed systematic differences in agency policy performance between higher and lower levels in a federal system. In particular, state public forests exhibit higher levels of management for timber outputs, economic profitability, and revenue sharing with local governments, whereas national public forests exhibit higher levels of management for environmental protection. Another performance measure, citizen participation, also differs systematically: Federal officials undertake greater efforts to encourage citizen participation than do state officials. Moreover, citizens who favor timber uses more actively participate in state forest policy, whereas citizens who favor environmental protection more actively participate in federal forest policy.

The most important contributing factor in these performance differences is the set of laws within which agency officials operate. Federal laws constrain federal forest bureaucrats' ability to provide timber and economic profitability more than state laws constrain state forest bureaucrats. At the same time, federal laws give citizens pursuing noneconomic benefits greater ability to intervene in federal forest policies than in state policies. In other words, laws created by elected officials are a powerful force shaping public policy, and the functional theory of federalism can be extended to bureaucrats. Elected officials behaving according to the functional theory create different legal constraints on agency members at different levels of governance, which in turn affect agency policy performance.

Laws do not tell the whole story, however. Other factors—such as agency membership, mobility of agency personnel, and geographic location of stakeholders, as described in bureaucratic behavior theory—affect patterns of citizen participation as well as policy outputs. Forest management plans also affect policy outputs.

Despite the important differences across levels of governance, several key factors do not differ systematically. Federal and state agency members do not differ substantially in their beliefs about appropriate forest management, nor are there discrete patterns in budgetary incentives. Moreover, state and federal agency communities do not exhibit systematically different levels of shared norms.

The remainder of this book proceeds as follows. Chapter 2 describes the forests examined in this analysis: four state-federal forest pairs in two different regions of the United States. Within each pair, forests share similar physical characteristics but fall into different government jurisdictions.

In chapter 3 the focus is on policy outputs, in the form of agency decisions about timber provision levels and associated fiscal results. I describe state and federal agency differences regarding timber sales, economic profit from timber provision, and transfer payments to local governments. State agencies provide substantially higher levels of timber, receive much larger unit profits, and transfer considerably more funds to local governments.

Chapter 4 examines environmental protection outputs. I use four criteria to measure the differences between state and federal agencies' environmental protection efforts: ecosystem-level management, rare species identification and protection, ecosystem research and monitoring, and soil and watershed protection and improvement. Federal officials undertake substantially greater efforts on these criteria than do state officials.

Chapter 5 describes differences in citizen participation patterns. Federal officials promote citizen participation in policymaking more than do state officials. In addition, participation varies across levels of government by interest type: Preservation proponents are more active in federal agency policymaking, whereas timber proponents are more active in state agency policymaking.

In chapter 6, the discussion turns to factors that affect agency policymaking. Bureaucratic behavior theory suggests four key factors, the first of which is rules. Two kinds of rules (laws and forest plan requirements) differ substantially by level of government. Federal laws and forest plans constrain the ability of officials to provide cost-effective timber more than do state laws and plans. At the same time, federal laws and plans promote multiple forest uses, especially environmental protection, and provide citizens greater power in decision making than do those at the state level.

Chapter 7 analyzes another kind of rule affecting bureaucratic behavior: budget incentives. Comparisons of appropriations, timber revenues, and other use-fee revenues reveal that, unlike the types of rules discussed in chapter 6, budget incentives do not exhibit systematic state-federal differences. Instead, across levels of government, the power of budget rules to influence agency officials' behavior is weakened by officials' perceived inability to change their budget allocations.

Chapter 8 investigates the three remaining factors affecting bureaucratic behavior: citizen pressure, agency officials' beliefs, and agency community. Systematic state-federal differences are evident in citizen pressure, with preservation interests wielding more influence at the federal level and timber interests wielding more influence at the state level. No systematic differences are evident, however, in agency officials' beliefs about appropriate forest management. Finally, the level of government is associated with two aspects of agency community: The federal agency community has members with longer employee tenure and relocation rates, along with a wider range of job positions. State and federal agency communities share similar levels of homogeneity of officials' beliefs within the agencies, however.

Chapter 9 draws on results from chapters 6–8 to explain the state-federal policy performance differences described in chapters 3–5. The most powerful explanatory factor across policy performance differences is rules, especially the laws created by elected officials. The National Forest Management Act, the National Environmental Policy Act, and the Multiple-Use, Sustained-Yield Act—all federal laws—limit national forest timber provision and economic returns through constraints on planning processes and on-the-ground activities. In particular, these laws empower citizens to block timber provision on national forests much more powerfully than they can on state forests.

Chapter 10 provides concluding comments. I summarize my findings and discuss implications for agency natural resource policy as well as for federalism more generally. I also extend the functional theory of federalism to nonelected bureaucrats via the influence of rules created by elected officials.

Note

1. Although Peterson originally (1981) focused on cities, his arguments can be applied to states, to the extent that migration is a viable option between states. For example, Greer (1979) and Orren (1974) argue that firms may use the threat of relocation to avoid state policies that would cost the firms significant amounts of money. Peterson subsequently (1995) argued that states occupy an intermediate position between the national and local governments with respect to the propensity to pursue developmental policies.

2 Comparing Four Forest Pairs

Green Blobs on a Map

If you look at a map of Indiana, you probably will get the impression that much of the state is flat farmland. You also might notice that there are quite a few green blobs sprinkled throughout the state, especially in the south. At first glance you might assume, as many people do, that all of these green blobs are state parks. On closer inspection, however, the markings reveal a more complicated picture. For example, if you examine the large green blob in south-central Indiana, not far from Bloomington, you might notice that it is demarcated into several distinct government jurisdictions, all adjacent: a state park, two different state forests, and a national forest.

If you are curious, you may wonder what importance, if any, a jurisdictional split has for the forest, its visitors, and the neighboring communities. If the green blobs on the map that are alike in geography also are alike in policy, it doesn't really matter which government jurisdiction is in charge. On the other hand, if government jurisdiction affects policy performance, questions about who should be in charge are of fundamental importance.

Although looking at green blobs on a map is a long way from a completed research project, it has been said that every long journey begins with a single step. The natural occurrence of different jurisdictions over neighboring forest areas sparked my interest in studying the questions I address in this book. I discovered that in many parts of the country it is common for forested areas to have multiple legal boundaries, each under a different government jurisdiction. Such areas make good "natural experiments" for testing ideas about how government jurisdiction affects policy performance, holding constant important physical characteristics related to geographic location.

Forest Differences and Similarities

My analysis draws on four forest pairs where a national forest is located in close proximity to a state forest system. The four pairs are in Ohio (Ohio state forests and Wayne National Forest), Indiana (Indiana state forests and Hoosier National Forest), Washington (Washington state forests and Gifford Pinchot National Forest), and Oregon (Oregon state forests and Siuslaw National Forest). Selection of these four forest pairs was based on two requirements: variation among the pairs and physical controls within each pair.

First, to discover general patterns in federal versus state forest policymaking, beyond the idiosyncrasies of a particular location, my analysis includes pairs in four different states. To increase the variation, I selected these states from two contrasting regions of the United States—the Midwest and the Pacific Northwest—that have substantially different types of forest ecosystems and quantities of forested land. Forests in these regions also differ with regard to contiguousness and the relative importance of the timber industry to state economies. These regional differences make it possible to test state-federal differences across diverse locations.

Second, to understand differences in policy performance relating to government jurisdiction rather than to physical characteristics of the forest, each pair has forests located in close proximity to one another and sharing similar physical characteristics. Although no two forests are identical, they can share key physical site characteristics that affect the forest ecosystem, including climate, topography, and soil type (Spurr and Barnes 1980: 108). These characteristics are linked to a forest's species composition and growth rate. In addition to controlling for physical characteristics, I controlled for time by collecting data from a single year: 1995.

Table 2.1. Midwest and Pacific Northwest Forests

	Region	
Characteristic	Midwest	Pacific Northwest
Primary forest type	Deciduous hardwood	Douglas fir/conifer
Quantity of forested land	20%–30% of land base	50% of land base
Forest contiguousness	Much fragmentation	Large contiguous blocks
Timber industry workforce	3,000–5,000 employees	20,000–25,000 employees

A commonality among all of the forests is the rich mix of policy processes, programs, and people. In the Midwest, although forests do not dominate the region's economy, several environmental interests and nontimber users compete with timber proponents who covet the region's valuable oak, maple, and other hardwood species. In the Pacific Northwest, the high importance of forests to the region and the salience of forest issues evident in endangered species debates and timber-cutting controversies indicate that a rich mix of processes and people is present. In each site, a large number of people have invested significant time and effort in affecting forest policy. Forest issues clearly are important to many people within and outside forest agencies in these four states.

Regional Differences

Several important differences are evident across the four forest pairs. Primary differences can be seen by comparing forests in Ohio and Indiana (in the Midwest) with forests in Washington and Oregon (in the Pacific Northwest). Specifically, these regions vary with regard to forest type, quantity of forested land, forest contiguousness, and timber industry size (see Table 2.1).

Forest type, which is identified by dominant tree species present, differs between the two regions. In the Midwest, the most common forest type is deciduous hardwood. The largest portion of timberland across Ohio is in the oak-hickory group, followed by the northern hardwoods group, which includes maple and beech species. Together these groups constitute about 84 percent of the state's timberland

(USDA Forest Service 1993a: 12–13). In Indiana, the dominant species group is maple-beech, followed by oak-hickory, which together total 71 percent of timberland in the state (USDA Forest Service 1990: 1–8). In the Pacific Northwest region, however, conifers dominate. The most common forest type in both Washington and Oregon is Douglas fir and associated conifers.

Quantity of forested land also differs between these regions. In Ohio, eight million acres of land are forested, which represents about 30 percent of total state land area. In Indiana, four million acres—about 20 percent of the state land area—are forested. There is a significantly higher quantity of forest land in the Pacific Northwest: In Washington about 20 million acres, or nearly 50 percent of the state, are forested, and in Oregon about 28 million acres—nearly 50 percent of the state's land base—are in forest cover (USDA Forest Service 1993c).

Not only do the states in the Pacific Northwest have a higher quantity of forest land, they also have more contiguous forest land. Large blocks of forested area are located throughout the mountainous regions in both states. This pattern is primarily a result of ownership history: Several U.S. presidents designated national forests on land that had not yet left the public domain. In the Midwest, the national forests were pieced together several decades later, from abandoned private holdings, on land that had been disposed of previously by the federal government.

Differences in forest resources are reflected in the timber industries in these regions. States in the Midwest have a substantially lower lumber and wood product value. In Ohio, lumber and wood production accounted for approximately $917 million in 1992, which was 0.4 percent of the gross state product. Similarly in Indiana, lumber and wood production in the same year were valued at $1,021 million, or 0.8 percent of gross state product. By contrast, lumber and wood production in Washington that same year totaled $3,078 million, or 4.9 percent of gross state product, and in Oregon these same industries accounted for $2,297 million, or 1.8 percent of gross state product (U.S. Department of Commerce 1995a). The higher timber production values in the Northwest also are reflected in workforce size. In 1992 personnel employed in logging and lumber mills totaled 24,600 in Washington and 20,300 in Oregon, compared to just 2,800 in Ohio and 5,100 in Indiana (U.S. Department of Commerce 1995b).

Physical Similarities within Forest Pairs

To compare the effects of forest management on timber sales and other forest benefits, it is necessary to control for the physical elements of the forest sites. For example, measuring the timber volume of a forest characterized by rich soil and a favorable climate against the timber volume of a forest with poor soil in a harsh environment would not provide a useful comparison of the effects of management activities on timber provision because physical factors would differ significantly. Two physical measures that combine soil type, climate, topography, and elevation characteristics are site productivity (the quantity of tree growth per acre per year) and forest type (dominant species). Within each of the four pairs, forests share similar physical characteristics with regard to these measures (see Table 2.2).

In the Ohio forests, site productivity is estimated to be approximately 150 board-feet[1] per acre per year on the state forests and about 144 board-feet per acre per year on the national forest. Another important similarity across the forests is dominant species. The most common forest types in this region are oak-hickory and northern hardwoods. Both the state forests and the national forests are predominantly of these types (USDA Forest Service 1993a).

In the Indiana forests, merchantable timber growth is estimated to be about 117 board-feet per acre per year on the state forests and 108 board-feet per acre per year on the national forest. Moreover, similar forest types have developed on state and national forest lands. The most common tree species groups in both places are oak-hickory and maple-beech (USDA Forest Service 1990).

In the Washington forests, tree species composition is similar across the state and national forests. The most common forest type on the national as well as the state forests is Douglas fir, which is found in association with western hemlock and western red cedar. Site quality also is similar across state and federal lands, although an important physical difference is the existence of significant patches of old-growth forest on the federal lands that are absent from the state lands. Unfortunately, neither the state agency nor the federal agency has information about the site productivity of its lands; no research studies exist that measure average annual growth quantities. Given the similarities

Table 2.2. Forest Pair Characteristics

Forest	Site Acreage	Productivity[a]	Forest Type (dominant species)
Ohio State Forests	176,787	150	Oak-hickory, northern hardwoods
Wayne National Forest	224,627	144	Oak-hickory, northern hardwoods
Indiana State Forests	144,110	117	Oak-hickory, maple-beech
Hoosier National Forest	180,209	108	Oak-hickory, maple-beech
Washington State Forests	2,100,000	—[b]	Douglas fir, western red cedar
Gifford Pinchot National Forest	1,075,879	—[b]	Douglas fir, western red cedar
Oregon State Forests	789,146	1,000	Douglas fir
Siuslaw National Forest	527,359	1,000	Douglas fir

[a] Estimated tree growth potential, measured in board-feet per acre per year.
[b] Data not available for this forest.

in geographical location and climate, however, one would expect that productive capacity across these forests does not differ dramatically.

Finally, in Oregon, state and national forest site productivity are similar, with both forests estimated to grow about 1,000 board-feet per acre per year. No substantial volume of old growth trees is present on either forest. In addition, tree species composition is similar across the state and national forests. The most common species in both places is Douglas fir.

Forest Ownership and Administration

Public forests are dynamic in many ways. Growth and change in their biological components are accompanied by growth and change in how they are owned and managed. The state and national forests that we see today in the United States are products of historical trends in land ownership and administrative structures.

In the early 1800s, as the youthful nation sought to expand its borders, the federal government acquired vast amounts of land through purchase (e.g., the Louisiana Purchase of 1803 added 560 million acres of land) and claims settlements (e.g., the Oregon Compromise and Mexican Treaty in the 1840s added more than 520 million acres) (Cubbage, O'Laughlin, and Bullock 1993: 285). As quickly as the country expanded its borders, however, policymakers sought to secure control by transferring ownership into private hands. For example, the Homestead Act of 1862 granted title of 160 acres to citizens willing to settle the land and cultivate it for at least five years.

In 1891 federal lawmakers passed the General Revision Act, which allowed for the reservation of land to be retained in the public domain for natural resource values. From that point on, federal efforts to transfer land into private hands occurred simultaneously with reservation to keep land in the public domain. In 1911, the Weeks Act empowered the federal government to purchase land from private owners to increase the public land base. The USDA Forest Service has continued to acquire forest lands over the years.

Meanwhile, state governments typically received title transfer of substantial federal land holdings when statehood was granted. Moreover, as private landowners failed to make tax payments during the Great Depression, many acres of land reverted to state ownership. To this day, state forest agencies have continued to expand state forest boundaries through land purchases.

By the first part of the twentieth century, federal and state governments owned land in sufficient quantities to warrant creation of administrative structures. Led by Gifford Pinchot, the federal forest management agency developed into a cadre of professional foresters with field and headquarters offices. Many states followed suit, creating state forester positions that grew into staffed forestry departments.

The forests described in this book reflect these historical patterns. State and national forests in Ohio, Indiana, Washington, and Oregon have grown over the years through land acquired and retained in the public domain. Administrative structures at the field and headquarters level are in place for agency officials to manage the forests.

Ohio State Forests and Wayne National Forest

The Ohio state forests and Wayne National Forest of today share a history of private ownership and cut-over conditions. In the mid-nineteenth century, people cleared large amounts of forest in Ohio for building material, fuel, and crop production. Harvesting targeted high-quality trees such as black walnut, cherry, and white oak, followed by other species, and many areas were burned repeatedly. By the turn of the twentieth century, few uncut areas remained in the state (Wayne National Forest 1996). This trend has reversed in the past several decades, however; in 1940 about 10 percent of the state was forested, but that figure has climbed to more than 30 percent today. The increase is largely a result of pasture land reverting, or being converted, to forest. A total of more than seven million acres is considered timberland;[2] more than 90 percent of this land is in private ownership, with the remaining portion in public (state or federal government agencies) ownership (USDA Forest Service 1993a: 9–10).

In Ohio, land acquisition for management by agency personnel began in the early part of the twentieth century. Government officials purchased formerly private land, much of it deforested and abused, and transferred it to public ownership. State officials first acquired land as state forest in 1916. Originally designed to create testing grounds for reforestation efforts, state land acquisition broadened to include land acquisition for scenic, recreational, and timber values. State officials acquired abandoned and abused lands to enlarge the state forest system, which has continued to grow over the years (Ohio Department of Natural Resources 1993). Meanwhile, the federal government experienced a similar land acquisition pattern. In 1934 the state legislature authorized the federal government to purchase damaged land to create the Wayne National Forest. In less than two decades, federal officials acquired more than 96,000 acres and designated the land as a national forest (Wayne National Forest 1996). Through the years, federal officials have continued to acquire land for the national forest.

By 1995, the state forest system included more than a dozen forests, totaling just more than 175,000 acres, most of which were located within a region of approximately 10,000 square miles. The national forest, which was close to 225,000 acres in size, contained several management units located primarily within the same region.

The state forest agency, which has responsibility for managing state forests, is a department headed by an appointed chief. The agency has a central office in Columbus (the state capital), as well as numerous field offices close to state forests. Although overall agency responsibilities include programs related to private forest land, in this study I focus on the agency's responsibilities for state-owned forests. The federal forest agency, as defined here, includes USDA Forest Service officials in the national forest's headquarters in Athens, Ohio, and in field offices who are responsible for managing the national forest.

Indiana State Forests and Hoosier National Forest

In Indiana, land-use history and ownership have followed a similar pattern as in Ohio. Today about 20 percent of the land area in the state is forested, most of which is considered timberland. Forested area has increased by approximately 10 percent since the mid-1960s. The increase is attributable to a reduced quantity of pastureland, along with restocking of lands that were cleared in the late 1800s and took a long time to recover because of highly erodible soils. Nearly 90 percent of the timberland is in private ownership; the remaining portion is in public ownership (federal, state, county, and municipal). The dominant forest type in Indiana is maple-beech—which constitutes about 38 percent of the total—followed by oak-hickory, which accounts for 33 percent of the total (USDA Forest Service 1990: 1–8).

Land acquisition in Indiana by the state and federal governments began in the early part of the twentieth century. State officials purchased land for the first state forest in 1903, but the majority of present-day state forests were purchased in the 1930s and 1940s (Ohio Division of Forestry 1995). Much of this land had been cleared for farming, and the state began by preventing erosion and restocking the forest to encourage reforestation. Federal officials first acquired land for the Hoosier National Forest in the midst of the Depression. As farmers abandoned deforested, marginally productive lands, local officials became concerned about rising property tax delinquency. The USDA Forest Service began to purchase land in the state in the mid-1930s and continued to do so over the following several decades.

By 1995 the state forest system included more than a dozen state forests, with a total of more than 140,000 acres. Nearly all of these forests are located within a 6,000 square mile area of the state. The national forest, which is divided into several districts, totaled about 180,000 acres. The national forest is located within the same region as the state forests, in an area of approximately 2,000 square miles.

The state forest agency responsible for managing state-owned forest lands is a division within the state's natural resources department, with headquarters in Indianapolis (the state capital). The forest agency is a distinct unit, with a central office in Indianapolis and numerous field offices near state forests. For comparative purposes, in this analysis I focus on the forest agency rather than the entire natural resources department. Moreover, although the agency has responsibilities relating to private forest land, I examine only its responsibilities relating to state-owned forests. For this analysis, the federal forest agency includes USDA Forest Service personnel at the national forest's headquarters in Bedford, Indiana, and in field offices who have management responsibilities for the national forest.

Washington State Forests and Gifford Pinchot National Forest

In Washington, the state became a forest land owner in 1889, when the federal government deeded land at statehood. The state expanded its ownership acreage in the 1930s by acquiring, from counties, land that had been logged and abandoned by private owners (Washington State Department of Natural Resources 1994). Meanwhile, the Gifford Pinchot National Forest was created as one of many "forest reserves" established by President Theodore Roosevelt at the turn of the twentieth century. First managed by the Department of the Interior, the forest was transferred to the Department of Agriculture before 1910. Land purchases and exchanges since then have adjusted the national forest's boundaries.

By 1995 the state forest system included more than a dozen state forests and numerous smaller patches of forested land—a total of about 2.1 million acres of forest land. These state forest lands are spread throughout the state, although most are located in an area of approximately 25,000 square miles in the western half of the state. The national forest, which is divided into four ranger districts, totals about 1.1 million acres of land. This forest is located within an area about 3,000 square miles in size, also located in the western half of the state.

The agency responsible for managing state-owned forest lands is a division within the state's natural resources department, with headquarters in the state capital, Olympia. I focus my analysis on the forest agency rather than the entire natural resources department. Although the state forest agency has responsibilities relating to private forest land, I concentrate on the agency's responsibilities for state-owned forests. The federal forest agency, as defined here, includes USDA Forest Service officials in the national forest's headquarters in Vancouver, Washington, and in field offices who are responsible for managing the national forest.

Oregon State Forests and Siuslaw National Forest

The first state-owned forest lands in Oregon were deeded by the federal government at statehood (in 1859). The state gained additional forest lands from private owners who lost title through tax foreclosure in the 1930s and then through purchase from counties following devastating forest fires in the 1930s, 1940s, and 1950s (Oregon Department of Forestry 1995). Meanwhile, the Siuslaw National Forest was created when President Theodore Roosevelt declared a large portion as "forest reserve" at the turn of the twentieth century. Federal officials acquired additional forest land as homesteaders abandoned scattered tracts in the 1930s (USDA Forest Service 1964).

By 1995 the state forest system included five state forests and numerous smaller patches of forested land—a total of nearly 800,000 acres of forest land (Oregon Department of Forestry 1995). These state forest lands are spread throughout the state, but more than two-thirds are concentrated in an area of approximately 1,600 square miles in the western half of the state. The national forest, which is divided into four ranger districts, totaled almost 530,000 acres. This forest is located within an area about 2,900 square miles in size, also in the western half of the state.

The state forest agency, which has responsibility for managing state forests, is a department headed by an appointed chief. The agency has a central office in the state capital, Salem, as well as numerous field offices close to state forests. Although the agency has responsibilities relating to private forest land, I focus on the agency's responsibilities over state-owned forests. The federal forest agency examined here includes USDA Forest Service officials in the national forest's headquarters in Corvallis, Oregon, and in field offices who are responsible for managing the national forest.

Conclusion

Most casual observers pay little attention to questions about government jurisdiction. Indeed, public forest lands may be regarded as undifferentiated green blobs on a map. In many places, however, the American landscape is demarcated by multiple government jurisdictions at different levels of government. Where such multiple jurisdictions share similar physical characteristics, we have the opportunity to study "natural experiments" of policy performance at different levels in a federal system.

The research presented in this book takes advantage of such natural experiments by examining four forest pairs. I chose the pairs from two dissimilar regions—the Midwest and the Pacific Northwest—to search for patterns in how the level of government affects policy performance. Within each pair, both forests share similar physical characteristics, but one is managed by the USDA Forest Service and the other is managed by a state forest agency. Consequently, my analysis highlights differences resulting from policymaking at different levels of government.

In the succeeding chapters, I describe the use of information from interviews, documents, and a questionnaire to compare state agency policy performance to federal agency policy performance (chapters 3–5) and factors affecting bureaucratic behavior (chapters 6–8), as well as to explain the differences I found (chapter 9). I turn to the first of the performance measures, timber provision and fiscal results, in chapter 3.

Notes

1. A board-foot is a standard measure of timber volume: one board-foot measures one foot by one foot by one inch.

2. Timberland refers to a forested area that is capable of producing at least twenty cubic feet of timber per acre per year and is not withdrawn from timber production.

Part Two

Differences in State and National Performance

3 State Agency Strengths:
Timber, Profits, and Revenue Sharing

The fundamental idea of forestry is the perpetuation of forests by use. Forest protection is not an end in itself; it is a means to increase and sustain the resources of our country and the industries which depend on them.

—Gifford Pinchot, *Breaking New Ground (1947)*

Yes, we need more conservation . . . but we also need an ample supply of all kinds of energy to prevent the price spikes that threaten our jobs and hurt our American families. . . . [Failing to develop energy sources] will give us shortages and high prices that endanger home ownership and kill job creation and destroy the American dream, because the American dream is fueled by energy, and we need it.

—Rep. John Peterson, in debate about opening
Arctic National Wildlife Refuge for oil exploration, August 1, 2001

Historically, the growth and development of the United States have been associated with making productive economic use of its bountiful natural resources. To this day, economic production is a prominent feature of any natural resource debate, from forests and fossil fuels to wilderness and wildlife.

Economic outputs are mentioned prominently by people who favor devolving greater authority from the federal level to the state level. As exemplified in stories of $400 hammers and $600 ashtrays procured by the Department of Defense, waste and inefficiency have long been attributed to the federal government. States, advocates of devolution argue, do a better job of providing cost-efficient services and promoting economic development. In public forest policy, productive economic use of forests can be measured in terms of timber sales quantities, as well as profitability and revenue sharing.

Timber Sales Volume

If you take a walk in the woods with a logger, you will hear about the important benefits of growing and harvesting timber. Properly managed, forests provide abundant, renewable resources for consumers. Trees are the raw material for thousands of products, from lumber and packaging material to the book you are holding in your hand. In an age of increasingly global trade, the United States has potential to produce substantial quantities of wood and wood products for consumers all over the world.

Of course, trees provide more than just consumer products. Timber sales fuel important economic development and employment opportunities with jobs that are relatively high paying in relation to their formal education requirements. It has been estimated that in the Pacific Northwest, every million board-feet of timber sold is linked to a dozen local jobs annually (Satchell 1996; Gilless et al. 1990). For many communities near rural forested areas, timber sales have provided a viable economic base over the years. This is especially true for timber from public forests, where government officials turn back a portion of timber sales revenue to nearby communities to fund roads, schools, and other public services.

In addition to consumer products and economic gains, tree growing and cutting can provide other benefits. For example, as trees grow they take in and store carbon, which reduces the atmospheric buildup of carbon dioxide, an important greenhouse gas. Carbon sequestration is greater in young, fast-growing trees than in older trees. Tree removal also can increase habitat diversity, promoting certain plants and animals.

Table 3.1. Volume of Timber Sold and Percent of Annual
Growth, 1995

Agency	Timber Sold (mmbf)[a]	Forest Size (acres)	Annual Estimated Growth (mmbf)	Share of Annual Est. Growth Sold (%)
Ohio				
State	5.4	176,787	27.6	19.6
Federal	1.5	224,627	32.3	4.6
Indiana				
State	3.2	144,110	17.0	18.8
Federal	1.0	180,209	19.4	5.1
Washington				
State	607.3	2,100,000	—[b]	—
Federal	45.8	1,075,879	—	—
Oregon				
State	126.6	789,146	789.1	16.0
Federal	8.9	527,359	527.4	1.7

[a] mmbf = million board-feet.
[b] Data not available for this forest.

Given the importance of timber production, it is appropriate to ask
whether state and federal public forests systematically differ in providing it. To answer this question, I collected information across all
eight forests, to gauge timber sales quantities as well as the portion
of each agency's budget that is directed toward timber provision.

As Table 3.1 shows, timber sales quantities differ dramatically by
level of government. In each of the four forest pairs, state forests provide substantially higher levels of timber outputs than do national
forests. This difference is apparent in total volume as well as the share
of tree growth sold.

In Table 3.1, the estimated annual growth rate for the forest as a
whole (fourth column) is calculated by multiplying the forest acres
(third column) by the average site productivity per acre (see Table
2.2). Numbers under 100 percent in the fifth column indicate that less
timber is being sold than is being added by tree growth.

Ohio state forest officials sold 5,415,472 board-feet of the estimated
27,600,000 board-feet of growth in fiscal year 1995, or 19.6 percent of
the growth. Wayne National Forest officials sold 1,500,000 board-feet

of the estimated 32,300,000 board-feet of growth in fiscal year 1995—just 4.6 percent of the growth.

Indiana state forest officials sold 3,200,000 board-feet, or 18.8 percent of the estimated 17,000,000 board-feet of growth in fiscal year 1995. The same year, Hoosier National Forest officials sold only 961,100 board-feet out of 19,400,000 board-feet estimated growth, which equals 5.1 percent of annual growth.

Washington state forest officials sold 607,300,000 board-feet in fiscal year 1995, while Gifford Pinchot National Forest officials sold just 45,800,000 board-feet. Unfortunately, no reliable estimate of annual growth across state or national forest lands exists in this state. However, comparison of timber volume sold, taking into account forested acreage, indicates that state officials provided more timber. The state forest land area was about twice the size of the national forest land area, yet state officials sold more than thirteen times as much timber volume as federal officials. Thus, on a per-acre basis, state officials sold a significantly higher amount of timber than did federal officials.

Oregon state forest officials sold 126,594,000 board-feet, or 16 percent of the estimated annual 789,100,000 board-feet of growth. Siuslaw National Forest officials sold 8,900,000 board-feet—just 1.7 percent of the estimated annual 527,400,000 board-feet of growth.

In each forest pair where data are available, officials at both agencies sold well below 100 percent of the annual growth; thus, they did not deplete the timber resource stock. In other words, these are sustainable harvest levels for the timber resource. The larger proportional volume of tree growth sold on state forests reflects greater timber provision by state than federal officials, however.

In addition to volume sold, we can compare the amount of emphasis agency officials place on timber provision relative to other activities. Here emphasis is indicated by agency financial resource allocation for timber provision. The portion of each agency's public forest management operating budget expended on timber provision is shown in Table 3.2.[1] In all four pairs, the state agency devoted a higher proportion of its resources toward timber provision than did the federal agency in fiscal year 1995.

Ohio state forest operating expenditures related to public forest management fall into six broad categories: timber management, for-

Table 3.2. Timber Expenditures, 1995

Agency	Timber Expenses[a]	Total Operating Expenses	Share of Operating Expenses (%)
Ohio			
State	$483,665	$4,489,019	10.8
Federal	211,868	3,739,628	5.7
Indiana			
State	73,166	2,548,991	2.9
Federal	69,295	3,642,007	1.9
Washington			
State	19,048,783	43,742,935	43.5
Federal	6,276,000	18,710,900	33.5
Oregon			
State	7,880,968	17,522,595	45.0
Federal	3,158,800	13,864,700	22.8

[a]Expenses for the Ohio, Washington, and Oregon forests include sale administration and timber growth management costs; in Indiana they include only sale administration costs (because of lack of data availability).

est operations, education and information, fire protection, law enforcement, and recreation. In fiscal year 1995, state timber management and sale expenditures were 10.8 percent of total operating expenditures for public forest management.

Wayne National Forest operating expenses related to public forest management include numerous line items, such as timber, fish, wildlife, recreation, ecosystem, soil and water, threatened species, general administration, law enforcement, fire, facilities maintenance, special uses, minerals, rangeland management, and road maintenance. Federal timber management and sale expenditures in Ohio in fiscal year 1995 were 5.7 percent of total operating expenditures for public forest management.

Indiana state forest operating expenditures related to public forest management are tracked in several functional categories, including personnel, utilities/postage, contracted services, fuel/office supplies, training, equipment, and travel. Field officers track expenses for each timber sale. Unlike in Ohio, state officials in Indiana do not track timber growth management expenses outside of particular sales. Thus, the only figures available for timber provision expenditures are those directly related to timber sales. In fiscal year 1995, timber sale expenses statewide represented about 2.9 percent of total operating expenditures for public forest management.

Hoosier National Forest operating expenditures related to public forest management are tracked in several dozen line items. For comparison with state timber sale expenses, federal timber sale expenditures used in analysis include timber sale expenses but not timber growth management activities outside of particular sales, which are excluded from state figures. In fiscal year 1995, Hoosier National Forest timber sale expenses were 1.9 percent of total operating forest expenditures for public forest management.

Washington state forest operating expenses are tracked biennially, so figures for fiscal year 1995 are best estimated by dividing biennial totals in half. Operating expenditures relating to public forest management include categories such as administration, financial services, leases, public use, forest management, timber sales, recreation, mapping, and engineering support, among others. In fiscal year 1995, state timber management and sale costs were 43.5 percent of the agency's total operating expenses for public forest management.

Gifford Pinchot National Forest operating expenditures are tracked in several dozen line items. In fiscal year 1995, expenses related to timber management and sales were 33.5 percent of the agency's total operating expenses for public forest management.

Oregon state forest operating expenditures relating to public forest management include administration, timber growth management, timber sales, miscellaneous land activity, engineering, recreation, and fire protection. Siuslaw National Forest operating expenditures relating to public forest management include similar activities in several dozen line items. In fiscal year 1995, state officials spent 45.0 percent of the agency's operating expenses for public forest management on timber management and sales. Meanwhile, federal officials spent 22.8 percent of the agency's operating expenses for public forest management on timber management and sales.

Across the forest pairs, then, expenditure data as well as sales quantity data reveal higher state emphasis on timber outputs. State officials sold higher timber volumes than did their federal counterparts in all four pairs. In so doing, they spent a higher proportion of their agency operating expenses on timber provision. Although timber expense proportions vary greatly between regions, in each pair the federal agency spent a lower proportion of its operating expenditures on timber provision.

Timber Sales Profitability

An important forest policy performance measure is the profitability of an agency's timber provision (Souder and Fairfax 1996: 99). Some scholars have argued that economic efficiency should be the primary goal of public forest management (see Krutilla and Haigh 1978). More generally, fiscal conservatives and taxpayer advocates often argue that when governments provide market goods, their operations should not incur economic losses.

The primary market good provided by forests is timber. Forest agencies incur costs in preparing timber for sale, and at the time of sale, the timber generates revenue. Comparing expenditures and revenues allows evaluation of an agency's net profit from timber provision. Across the eight forests in this analysis, fundamental differences exist between state and federal agency performance on this measure. State forest agency officials provide much more profitable timber than do federal forest agency officials.

As is common for public forests in the United States, agency personnel in the eight forests at hand generally do not conduct harvesting operations themselves. Instead, they sell the right to harvest timber to private contractors who bid for individual sales, called "stumpage." Each successful contract bidder agrees to pay a specified price and abide by harvesting conditions described in a sale contract. The agency's net profit on a sale is calculated by subtracting the costs of sale administration and timber growth management from the stumpage sale price.[2] The agency's net profit per unit of output is measured by comparing costs and revenues per board-foot (see Table 3.3).

For the Ohio forest pair, timber cost data in each agency are available for sale administration and timber growth management activities. For fiscal year 1995, Ohio state forest officials sold timber at a lower

Table 3.3. Timber Revenues and Costs, 1995

Agency	Timber Costs[a]	Timber Revenues	Volume (mmbf)	Unit Costs (per bf)	Unit Revenues (per bf)	Unit Profit (per bf)
Ohio						
State	$483,665	$2,106,247	5.4	$0.09	$0.39	$0.30
Federal	211,868	153,569	1.5	0.14	0.10	−0.04
Indiana						
State	73,166	854,561	3.2	0.02	0.27	0.25
Federal	69,295	17,575	1.0	0.07	0.02	−0.05
Washington						
State	19,048,783	285,300,000	607.3	0.03	0.47	0.44
Federal	6,276,000	15,130,332	45.8	0.14	0.33	0.19
Oregon						
State	7,880,968	64,165,957	126.6	0.06	0.51	0.45
Federal	3,158,800	2,882,790	8.9	0.35	0.32	−0.03

[a]For Ohio, Washington, and Oregon, state and federal costs include administration activities associated with timber sales (e.g., tree marking, road layout, sale advertising, and contract administration) as well as timber-management activities outside particular sales (e.g., pruning and weed control). For Indiana, only sale administration activities are included in state and federal costs because of accounting methods in the state agency.

cost per board-foot than did Wayne National Forest officials. Timber costs on state forests totaled $483,665 to provide 5,415,472 board-feet, which equals $0.09 per board-foot. Timber expenses on the national forest totaled $211,868 to provide 1,500,000 board-feet, or $0.14 per board-foot.

For the Indiana forest pair, timber costs include sale administration activities but not timber growth management activities because the state did not track the latter expenses. Timber costs on Indiana state forests were $73,166 to provide 3,200,000 board-feet, which equals $0.02 per board-foot. Timber costs on the Hoosier National Forest were considerably higher, totaling $69,295 for 961,100 board-feet, or $0.07 per board-foot.

For the Washington forest pair, timber costs include sale administration and timber growth management activities. Timber costs on

Washington state forests totaled $19,048,783 to provide 607,300,000 board-feet, or $0.03 per board-foot. Timber costs were higher on Gifford Pinchot National Forest: $6,276,000 to provide 45,800,000 board-feet, or $0.14 per board-foot.

For the Oregon forest pair, timber costs include sale administration and timber growth management activities. Timber costs on Oregon state forests totaled $7,880,968 to provide 126,594,000 board-feet, or $0.06 per board-foot. Timber costs on Siuslaw National Forest were substantially higher: $3,158,800 to provide 8,900,000 board-feet, or $0.35 per board-foot.

Thus, federal agency timber sales in all four pairs exhibited higher unit costs; at the same time, they generated significantly lower unit revenues. For fiscal year 1995, Ohio state forest revenue from timber sales totaled $2,106,247, from the sale of 5,415,472 board-feet, or $0.39 per board-foot. Timber sales on Wayne National Forest generated $153,569 from the sale of 1,500,000 board-feet, yielding revenues of only $0.10 per board-foot.

Indiana state forest revenue from timber stumpage sold totaled $854,561. This revenue came from 3,200,000 board-feet, for an average of $0.27 per board-foot. Hoosier National Forest timber sales, on the other hand, earned just $17,575 from 961,000 board-feet, yielding $0.02 per board-foot.

Washington state forest officials earned $285,300,000 from the sale of 607,300,000 board-feet of timber, for an average revenue of $0.47 per board-foot. Gifford Pinchot National Forest officials, on the other hand, earned $15,130,332 from the sale of 45,800,000 board-feet, or just $0.33 per board-foot.

Oregon state forest revenue was $64,165,957 from the sale of 126,594,000 board-feet, or $0.51 per board-foot. On Siuslaw National Forest, officials earned $2,882,790 from the sale of 8,900,000 board-feet—only $0.32 per board-foot.

With lower costs and higher revenues, state timber sales generated significantly higher profits than did sales on the national forests. In Ohio, state unit profits were $0.39 − $0.09 = $0.30 per board-foot, whereas national forest timber sales generated a net loss: $0.10 − $0.14 = −$0.04 per board-foot (see Table 3.3). In Indiana, state unit profits were $0.27 − $0.02 = $0.25 per board-foot, whereas national forest sales generated a net loss: $0.02 − $0.07 = −$0.05 per board-foot. In Washington, state unit profits were $0.47 − $0.03 = $0.44, whereas national forest sales generated a unit net profit of only $0.33 − $0.14 = $0.19. In Oregon, state unit profits were $0.51 − $0.06 = $0.45 per board-foot, compared to a net loss on the national forest: $0.32 − $0.35 = −$0.03 per board-foot.

Revenue Sharing

Besides agency profitability of operations, another important economic issue in public forest management is its impact on local tax bases. Unlike most private lands, public lands are not subject to property taxes. For jurisdictions such as counties and school districts whose primary revenue source is property tax, there is concern that public lands deprive these jurisdictions of crucial tax resources. In several states, USDA Forest Service attempts to purchase land to increase the size of a national forest have faced fierce local opposition because residents fear their local governments will suffer tax base reductions.

To address the local tax base issue, public lands are subject to various revenue-sharing policies, whereby a portion of revenues earned on public lands will be transferred to local governments (e.g., counties, townships, school districts, or other jurisdictions). Among the eight forests I examined for this book, state forests provide substantially higher levels of transfer payment to local governments than do national forests (see Table 3.4).

In Ohio, state law requires Ohio state forest officials to share 50 percent of net timber and oil/gas/mineral revenues with the county and township of origin. For timber costs, accountants track expenses to a timber management charge code, which includes equipment and personnel costs, for a given fiscal year. They add a charge of 15 percent (to account for a share of agency overhead costs) to generate total timber costs, which they subtract from total timber revenues to yield a net timber profit figure for revenue-sharing purposes. For oil/gas/mineral profit sharing, the agency does not track costs specific to oil/gas/minerals. Instead, revenues are multiplied by 90 percent to determine net profit. Net profit values from timber and oil/gas/minerals are combined to yield net commodity profit, which is divided

Table 3.4. Revenue-Sharing Transfers, Forest Agency to
Counties and Townships, 1995

Agency	Accrued to Counties[a]	Forest Size (acres)	Accrued per acre
Ohio			
State	$721,769	176,787	$4.08
Federal	15,554	224,627	0.07
Indiana			
State	120,867	144,110	0.84
Federal	13,755	180,209	0.08
Washington			
State	36,669,172	623,000	58.86
Federal	11,287,603	1,075,879	10.49
Oregon			
State	31,803,700	654,991	48.56
Federal	13,087,100	527,359	24.81

[a]For state agencies with legal trust mandates (Washington and Oregon), dollar and acreage figures include forest land held in trust for the counties, not those held in trust for other beneficiaries (e.g., common school fund).

equally between the state general fund and the county and townships from which the commodity was derived. For fiscal year 1995, Ohio state forest officials generated $721,769 ($719,015 from timber plus $2,754 from oil/gas/minerals) for county and township governments across the state. Taking forest size into account, this figure amounts to about $4.08 per acre (see Table 3.4).

Federal forest officials in Ohio also faced legal requirements that specify revenue-sharing with local governments. The federal Twenty-Five Percent Fund (16 USCA 500) requires that 25 percent of gross revenues that the forest agency receives from forest products and other user payments must be paid to the state in which the national forest is located, to be distributed to the county from which the revenues were generated. Wayne National Forest officials generated $15,554 for payment to county governments with land in the national forest.[3] This figure amounts to just $0.07 per acre.

Revenue-sharing requirements in Indiana resemble those in Ohio. Indiana state forest officials share 15 percent of net timber profit with local governments. Agency officials on state forests prepare cost summary sheets for each sale, including items such as tree marking, administration, boundary location, advertising, and equipment for road work. Officials subtract these costs from the winning bid revenue to determine net profit from each timber sale. The state forest system shared $120,867 with counties in fiscal year 1995, or $0.84 per acre. Meanwhile, as in Ohio, federal officials in Indiana shared 25 percent of gross (not net) revenues for timber and other forest revenues with the county from which they derived the revenues. This formula yielded a total of just $13,755, or $0.08 per acre, transferred from the Hoosier National Forest to county coffers.

In Washington, state forest officials manage state-owned lands in trust for several different beneficiaries, including schools, colleges, universities, and counties. For comparison with federal revenue sharing, analysis focuses on state payments to counties. Counties receive, on average, 35 percent of gross revenue earned on state forests located within their boundaries. In fiscal year 1995, counties earned $36,669,172, or $58.86 per acre, from state forest land revenues.

On the Gifford Pinchot National Forest in Washington, the 1993 Interior and Related Agencies Appropriations Act (IRAA) altered the standard 25 percent payment to counties from national forest gross revenues. Counties affected by harvesting restrictions related to northern spotted owl protection were entitled to receive the greater of either 25 percent of national forest revenues or a variable percentage (82 percent in fiscal year 1995) of the 1986–1990 average annual payment. In fiscal year 1995, the latter formula provided a larger sum, and $11,287,603, or $10.49 per acre, accrued to counties in which the national forest is located.

In Oregon, as in Washington, state forest officials manage state-owned lands in trust for counties and schools. Again, the analysis here focuses on transfer payments to counties. On lands managed for the benefit of counties, Oregon state forest officials transfer 63.75 percent of all revenues earned to the counties in which the forest is located. In fiscal year 1995, this formula generated $31,803,700, or $48.56 per acre, for counties.

On the national forest in Oregon, IRAA required officials to transfer to counties the greater of 25 percent of revenues earned or 82 percent of the annual average transferred between 1986 and 1990.

Federal officials generated $13,087,100, or $24.81 per acre, for counties.

Conclusion

The use of natural resources for economic development is a long-standing tradition in the United States. Timber is an important forest product that can spur economic development and bolster local economies. For publicly owned forests, my analysis reveals that economic development performance varies by level of government jurisdiction. Systematic differences between state and federal forest policy are evident in timber sales volume, as well as timber profitability and revenue sharing with local governments.

State agency officials provide substantially higher timber volumes than do their federal counterparts. In each forest pair, state officials sold a higher volume and devoted a greater share of agency operating expenditures to timber provision. In the three pairs where timber growth potential has been estimated, timber sale volumes at both forests were substantially below the estimated annual growth (e.g., between 1.7 percent and 19.6 percent of annual growth), so no agency was depleting its stock of timber. In each of these pairs, however, state officials sold a significantly higher proportion of annual growth than did federal officials.

Economic performance also differs systematically. Proponents of policy devolution in a federal system often cite expected gains in efficiency or cost savings as a reason for granting greater responsibilities to lower levels of governance. Evidence from the eight forests supports this claim; state agencies generate higher economic profits from timber provision than do federal agencies.

Another important economic measure is revenue sharing with local governments. Counties receive larger revenue-sharing payments from state forests than from national forests. This result informs an important issue in intergovernmental relations. Officials in local government jurisdictions have reason to be concerned about land in their county that is in public ownership because such land does not provide property tax revenue. To compensate for lost property tax revenues, public land management agencies share their revenues with local governments. Such sharing is not equal across levels of governance, however; in the forest pairs examined here, local governments receive much higher fund transfer levels from state lands than from national lands. This state-federal difference results from the revenue-sharing formulas that link revenue sharing to timber sales revenue or net profit, both of which are greater on state forests than on national forests.

Notes

1. Some of the agencies' expenditures are related to private forest land—for example, programs to help private forest owners reduce the threat of forest fires. Such expenditures that are not related to public forest management are separated so that the analysis captures only the public forest management aspect of agency responsibilities.

2. Costs to provide timber can be grouped into two categories: sale administration and timber growth management. The first category includes costs associated with particular timber sales, including marking trees, soliciting and evaluating bids, meeting with purchasers, administering contracts, and monitoring for contract compliance. The second category includes labor and materials used to promote growth of trees for future timber. Common timber growth management activities include "cruises" to establish inventory levels, as well as timber stand improvement tasks such as pruning trees, cutting vines, and removing competing vegetation. In this second category, expenses are not matched with specific timber sales. For example, vine-cutting costs in year 1 for trees that will be harvested in year 2 are tracked as timber management costs in year 1, even though revenue from those particular trees will be counted in year 2 (officials generally do not track expenses to the degree that would be necessary for accrual to a particular tree over the life of the tree). Nevertheless, I include timber growth management figures here to provide the most accurate estimate of total costs associated with timber provision.

3. Counties also receive payments from statutory Payments in Lieu of Taxes (PILT) from national forests located within the county. Because these payments depend solely on statute rather than forest officials' activities, however, I exclude them from this analysis. Even if they were included, the total transfers from the national forest and unit would still be far less than the totals from the state forests. For example, PILT payments in Ohio totaled $129,096, or $0.58 per acre, in fiscal year 1995.

4 Federal Agency Strength:
Environmental Protection

Some species of trees have been "read out of the party" by economics-minded foresters because they grow too slowly, or have too low a sale value to pay as timber crops. . . . [But] a system of conservation based solely on economic self-interest is hopelessly lopsided.

—Aldo Leopold, *A Sand County Almanac,* 1949

There are simply places on earth that are too fragile, too vulnerable and too special really to drill for oil. We have a real moral obligation to protect these places. . . . Pillaging the Arctic will not solve our energy problems. It will, however, endanger precious habitat and wilderness. . . .

—Rep. Barbara Lee, in debate about opening
Arctic National Wildlife Refuge for oil exploration,
August 1, 2001

The debate over oil exploration in the Arctic National Wildlife Refuge highlights persistent tensions between economic development and environmental protection of natural resources. There are fundamentally different beliefs among policymakers, as well as within the American public, about the appropriate purposes and uses of natural resources. In public forest policy, proponents of using timber for economic development are countered by those who argue that public forests should be managed primarily for environmental protection.

If you take a walk in the woods with an environmental advocate, you will hear about the important benefits of preserving the forest ecosystem. Protected forests can provide a multitude of benefits for people, from medicine and food to solitude and exercise. In fact, with the rapidly growing popularity of outdoor recreation, one can argue that the most-valued consumer forest use today is not timber but recreational opportunities. Less directly, humans benefit from environmental services such as water purification, wildlife habitat, and soil stability that forests provide. Beyond benefits to humans, some people believe that forests and their plant and animal inhabitants have intrinsic values—and as such the right to exist regardless of their contributions to human well-being.

Even among people who advocate timber cutting, minimizing environmental harm is an important goal. Like any other forest benefit, timber depends on healthy forests. As our understanding of environmental interconnections deepens, it is becoming quite evident that forest health includes more than just the protection of trees from wildfires, pests, and diseases. An underlying condition that is necessary for sustainable forest uses is a healthy forest ecosystem. Thus, environmental protection of forests is an important policy performance measure.

In the context of federal systems, environmental protection provides a useful area in which to compare differences in policy performance across levels of governance. Although environmental protection does not always conflict with economic development, in many instances efforts to increase environmental protection preclude certain economic development opportunities. This is especially true for timber cutting, which has substantial potential for environmental harm. Tradeoffs between environmental protection and economic development can be linked to the functional theory of federalism, which suggests that elected officials at lower levels of governance are less likely than those at higher levels to forgo economic development. In my analysis, comparison across the forest pairs allows testing of the functional theory on agency policymakers.

Comparing Environmental Protection

Ideally, policy analysis focusing on environmental protection would include direct measures of ecological conditions at specific sites. Measuring ecological conditions directly is beyond the scope of this book, however (in fact, entire manuscripts have been devoted to examining small portions of forest ecosystems, even a single tree). Moreover, ecological conditions depend largely on microclimate and other microlevel conditions, which cannot be held constant across forests.

Instead, the research at hand focuses on forest officials' efforts to promote environmental protection. I examine data to compare agency officials' environmental protection outputs—the extent of their efforts to protect the forest environment.

Environmental protection efforts are not as easy to measure as timber sales quantities or fiscal results. Experts disagree not only about which management activities lead to healthier forest ecosystems but also about what healthy forest ecosystems look like. No single indicator can measure environmental protection efforts fully, but several indicators, taken together, do provide a multidimensional picture of environmental protection. I use four indicators for this analysis: ecosystem-level management, rare species identification and protection, ecosystem research and monitoring, and soil and watershed protection and improvement. On the basis of these indicators, I find that federal officials provide more extensive efforts to promote environmental protection than do state officials (see Table 4.1).

Ecosystem-Level Management

Management at the ecosystem level, rather than on a species or stand basis, is one indicator of effort to increase environmental protection. Ecosystem-level management involves integrated, holistic thinking and planning for ecological communities rather than for single species. As forestry professor Jerry Franklin argues, holistic thinking is required to overcome the high expense and lack of knowledge that impede humans' ability to manage effectively on a species-by-species basis (Franklin 1993: 130). Because many species have yet to be discovered,[1] and our understanding of complex interactions among species is limited, it is important to focus on the ecosystem level.

Table 4.1. Comparison of Environmental Protection Efforts

	Agency with Greater Environmental Protection Efforts			
Indicator	Ohio	Indiana	Washington	Oregon
Ecosystem-level management	Federal	Federal	Federal	Federal
Rare species	Federal	Federal	Federal	Federal
Ecosystem research / monitoring	Federal	Federal	Federal	Federal
Soil and watershed Protection	Similar	Similar	Similar	Similar
Improvement	Federal	Federal	Federal	—[a]

[a] Data not available (state agency does not track).

In the past decade, a shift in federal public forest policy has included support for ecosystem management, which is defined as a process that involves the "integrated use of ecological knowledge at various scales to produce desired resource values, products, services and conditions in ways that also sustain the diversity and productivity of ecosystems" (USDA Forest Service 1993b). Rather than focusing management efforts on a particular stand of trees or type of human benefits, planning overtly includes other aspects of the forest community, including soils, hydrology, plants, and animals.

To compare ecosystem-level management across levels of government, I collected information about planning processes at each agency. The data show that federal agency officials practice ecosystem-level management to a greater degree than do state agency officials. Although officials at both levels consider a variety of ecosystem impacts in their management prescriptions, in all four pairs the federal agency performs more extensive, interdisciplinary analysis than does the state agency.

Ohio State Forests

In Ohio, vegetative manipulation at the state level begins with a forester's "cruise." An Ohio state forest official gathers data from at least ten plots in each stand (a relatively homogeneous area of trees, typically 20 to 50 acres in size, though sometimes as large as 100 acres). Plot data emphasize tree species, quantity, basal area, age, and merchantable volume, as well as the frequency of grape vines that reduce timber value. In addition, the forester makes notes about any unusual cultural sites, species, soil conditions, or other features. The forester prepares a "cruise report," recommending either no current action, a timber sale, or timber stand improvement activities such as cutting of vines. The report typically does not involve interdisciplinary consultation with other personnel.

If the report prescribes a timber sale, the forester checks a state rare species database (maintained by a different state agency) to see if any rare species are listed in the vicinity. One state official cited an example in which finding a rare species affected timber harvest plans. Another state official downplayed the impact of such findings on management operations, however, contrasting his agency with federal agency procedures: "I think that when an agency like the Forest Service has botanists, zoologists, and other such specialists, they go out of their way to make rare species a big deal. . . . Here, rare species have not really affected our management activities."

The forester's supervisor receives the cruise report and has responsibility for its approval. The supervisor routinely approves reports that do not indicate potential problems, but sometimes the supervisor may make a field visit. For example, one timber sale recommendation near a horse trail led to a field visit and subsequent talk with a horse riders' group to inform members of the timber sale plans. For most cruise reports that do not recommend a timber sale, the process ends with the report being filed for future reference. For a report that recommends a timber sale, however, the supervisor sends it to the forest agency headquarters for approval at the next higher level.

At the headquarters, an official checks the prescription to see if the proposed harvest will enhance timber growth. The official also looks for potential problems. If the official approves the sale, he or she will send out bid notices to seek a purchaser of the right to harvest the timber.

Wayne National Forest

In Ohio, forest management activities at the federal level involve a higher degree of ecosystem analysis and interdisciplinary work. In the past, analysis focused only on the stand level—an area of about 500 to 1,000 acres. Now, however, before the forester's cruise, Wayne National Forest officials complete an "opportunity area analysis" covering 10,000 to 60,000 acres, including land outside national forest boundaries. Concurrently, officials conduct an environmental assessment. These planning efforts involve an interdisciplinary team that analyzes a wide variety of components, including cultural resources (archaeologist), biological resources (wildlife biologist, fisheries biologist, and botanist), visual quality objectives (landscape architect), soil and water resources (hydrologist and soil scientist), vegetative management (silviculturist), recreation (recreation planner), public involvement (public affairs officer), and transportation systems (civil engineer).

The forester's cruise takes place within the broader planning of the opportunity area analysis and environmental assessment. Like state forest management cruising, national forest management cruising focuses on information about trees. Officials collect plot data to tally tree species, size, age, and merchantable volume. The cruise also includes information about slope direction and steepness (topographic characteristics), seed production, and soil drainage. Officials note additional information regarding cultural features, exotic species, and previous land degradation.

After the environmental assessment and opportunity area analysis have been completed and provided for public comment, the deciding officer publishes a decision notice and then waits until the forty-five-day appeal period has ended. If no appeals are made, the timber sale can be put up for bid.

Indiana State Forests

In Indiana, at the state level a long-term harvest schedule designates which forest areas are to be harvested in which years, according to timber maturity and stocking (timber volume) levels. In a given forest area, vegetative manipulation begins with a timber cruise. An Indiana state forest timber resource specialist examines one plot point per two acres in the area scheduled to be inventoried. For each tree, the official collects data on species, diameter, height, and proportion of the tree that is of "sound" log grade. For the stand of trees the official records information about slope direction and steepness, location in management tract, timber type, timber stocking level, tree mortality, and presence of vines. Finally, the official notes any rare species, including those in the understory. If the official finds a rare species, he or she notifies the state agency responsible for nature preserves to obtain advice about how to protect the species. One resource specialist said he had found rare species only "a couple of times" over the past few years.

Next, a state resource specialist uses the tree data to write a report and prescription for each forest area. If the stocking level is above a certain amount indicated for "good forestry" and if the trees are old enough to be attractive to prospective bidders, the specialist prescribes a harvest. In such cases, the specialist next notifies the state agency that is responsible for historic preservation, which checks the area for old home sites and prehistoric artifacts.

Subsequently, the specialist marks which trees in the harvest area are to be cut. The specialist also lays out logging roads and schedules equipment to build them. Seeding and water diversion devices are used on the roads to reduce erosion. Then the local office sends notices to potential bidders.

Hoosier National Forest

Timber sales on the national forest in Indiana involve broader analysis than do sales on state forests. Like their federal counterparts in Ohio, Hoosier National Forest officials first perform opportunity area analyses. Interdisciplinary teams examine a landscape-scale area (usually 1,000 to 10,000 acres) to identify the resource base as well as existing uses. Hoosier National Forest officials use the completed opportunity area analysis to generate a list of potential projects (e.g., habitat work, soil improvement, trails, timber, cultural resources) from which to set priorities.

Like state officials, federal officials in Indiana complete timber cruises. Cruises on the national forest, however, occur within a broader context of resource examination by archaeologists, biologists, and botanists. Hoosier National Forest officials use data to prepare alternatives for public comment and evaluation in an environmental assessment. If no appeals are submitted within the decision period, the sale is put up for bid as scheduled.

Washington State Forests

In Washington, state officials begin the timber sale process with a five-year timber plan. The plan guides which stands on Washington state forests are to be cut during which time period, based on stocking levels, commercial value, and desired stand conditions. On the basis of the plan, northern spotted owl and marbled murrelet survey needs are determined, to avoid a "take" under the Endangered Species Act. Where required, such survey crews complete the bird surveys prior to the timber sale. In addition, officials may complete a watershed analysis, which involves a landscape-level review of water quality, fish, erosion hazards, and other items. Watershed analyses are not required, however.

Next, the unit forester holds a preharvest review before marking the sale boundary, designing roads, and cruising stands to estimate volume. Before preparing a final sale notification and contract, state officials must complete two additional forms. The first is a State Environmental Policy Act (SEPA) checklist, which includes information about slope, soils, water quality and runoff, vegetation and wildlife, threatened or endangered species known to be near the site, environmental health hazards, aesthetics, recreational uses, and cultural sites. It is important to note, however, that checklist completion usually is not an interdisciplinary endeavor. In fact, checklist instructions to the forester state, "In most cases you should be able to answer the questions from your own observations or project plans without the need to hire experts." The second required form is a Forest Practices Act (FPA) application, which includes information about riparian areas, wetlands, road construction, harvest methods, and reforestation.

Once these two forms are approved, the unit forester provides a complete sale proposal packet to the state agency's headquarters, for approval by a higher agency official. If the proposed sale is more than twenty acres and $100,000 in appraised value—as most are—it also must be approved by the Board of Natural Resources. An agency representative presents such sales to the board on a monthly basis. Most proposed sales are approved by the board, which is composed primarily of representatives of trust funds that receive income from timber sales. Subsequently, the sale is put up for bid.

Gifford Pinchot National Forest

In Washington, timber sales on the national forest go through an even higher level of comprehensive analysis than do those on the state forests. Long-term timber plans are included in the Gifford Pinchot National Forest Land and Resource Management Plan—a document that describes supply, management direction, and goals for forest resources such as timber, recreation, wildlife, old growth forest, scenery, water quality, native plant communities, wild and scenic rivers, and air quality. As in other national forests, officials here complete interdisciplinary analyses as part of the environmental assessment process prior to putting a timber sale up for bid. A team of specialists in planning, soil science, hydrology, wildlife, fisheries, silviculture, engineering, geology, and sometimes archaeology gathers information and conducts surveys on a wide range of forest resources.

In addition to the comprehensive analysis for an environmental assessment, federal officials also must prepare interdisciplinary watershed analyses in areas designated as key watersheds, roadless areas, and riparian reserves. These analyses include information about the watershed's historic and current conditions, capacity, and range of vegetation. Federal officials go beyond minimum requirements for preparing watershed analyses, conducting such analyses for parts of the forest outside the areas in which watershed analyses are required.

Oregon State Forests

In Oregon, state agency long-range plans traditionally focused on estimated timber sales volumes. As one official explained, "These forest plans were really timber management plans, without specific planning for other resources." Planned timber sale targets were adjusted through input from unit foresters, who identified conditions on the ground that affected harvest potential. In fiscal year 1995, these traditional long-range plans were being changed, and unit foresters were gaining an increasingly important role in determining timber sales. For example, unit foresters select candidate areas for harvest. As one such official described it,

> To select potential harvest units, I balance economic and silviculture factors. Rotation age for regeneration harvesting is typically seventy years on this district, especially for sites with single species and low vertical diversity. For thinning, we aim for thirty-five-year-old stands.

The unit forester prepares a sale proposal, which addresses wildlife and fish resources and, if there are specific concerns, soils and road building issues. Each unit sale plan is reviewed by a wildlife biologist from outside the forest agency, who focuses on Endangered Species Act requirements for listed species. Forest officials also may ask outside fisheries biologists for consultation if a stream is present within the proposed sale area.

The unit forester submits the completed unit sale proposal to the state agency's central office, where officials review the proposal and combine it with plans from other units into a statewide annual sale plan. Central office officials subsequently compile a quarterly list of all impending timber sales, including information about bidding. Each district manages the sealed bidding process for local timber sales, awarding the sale to the highest bidder.

Thus, for the state agency in Oregon, analysis prior to timber sales focuses on a stand level rather than a landscape level. Moreover, comprehensive planning generally is limited to consultation with wildlife, fisheries, and perhaps soil specialists outside the agency, rather than a wide-ranging interdisciplinary agency team. In fact, long-range plans traditionally have focused on timber, not other forest resources. It is important to note, however, that at the time of this study state officials were in the process of creating a new long-range planning process that would provide more comprehensive analysis prior to timber sales. The impetus for this new approach was a desire to gain greater certainty in timber sales in the face of Endangered Species Act restrictions related to the northern spotted owl, marbled murrelet, and possibly (in the future) some salmon species. The state was developing a Habitat Conservation Plan that, if approved by the U.S. Fish and Wildlife Service and the National Marine Fisheries Service, would ensure continued timber sales even in areas where listed species exist. The new planning process would support the Habitat Conservation Plan. Thus, a more integrated, holistic planning process was spurred by a federal legal requirement (the Endangered Species Act).

Siuslaw National Forest

In Oregon, as in the other forest pairs, federal officials perform more extensive, interdisciplinary analysis prior to timber sales than do state officials. The Siuslaw National Forest Land and Resource Management Plan addresses not only timber but also resources such as recreation, visual resources, wildlife habitat, watershed condition, research opportunities, and cultural resources.

Before proposing a timber sale, federal officials prepare environmental assessments with the input of an interdisciplinary team of agency specialists in a variety of fields. They also prepare either a landscape-level watershed analysis or a "late successional reserve assessment," depending on the management area where the proposed activity will take place. These efforts generate information about a wide range of resources so that officials are able to manage for the forest ecosystem rather than just for timber.

Summary

Overall, as measured by degrees of ecosystem-level management, federal agency officials in all four pairs undertake greater environmental protection efforts than do state officials. Differences are large in the Midwest pairs, where state officials traditionally have not performed landscape-level, interdisciplinary analyses prior to timber sales. Differences are less pronounced in the Pacific Northwest, where state officials focus on certain nontimber resources before completing timber sales. Even in these forests, however, federal officials provide a higher degree of interdisciplinary analysis to support ecosystem-level management.

Rare Species Identification and Protection

Environmental protection includes concern for all of the species that interact in a forest ecosystem. Many organisms contribute to the complex web of life in ways that are not well understood; the loss of one or a few key species potentially can cause a chain reaction that affects the health of the entire forest (Roush 1989). Thus, environmental protection in the context of forest management includes identification and protection of rare species. In talking with agency officials and comparing activity reports and budget allocations, I found that federal officials undertake proactive measures to identify and protect rare species to a greater degree than do state officials.

Ohio

In Ohio, federal officials performed more rare species identification and protection efforts than did state officials. In addition to biological analyses for environmental assessments and opportunity area analyses, as described above, Wayne National Forest officials performed other activities aimed at identifying and protecting rare species. In fiscal year 1995, federal officials completed numerous such projects, including monitoring the population of a regionally sensitive sparrow and developing a management plan to enhance habitat for that species. Federal officials also contributed to an ongoing, joint effort with the U.S. Fish and Wildlife Service and a university to monitor migratory songbird abundance and species richness. Other monitoring efforts aimed to provide information about certain species, for possible addition to rare species lists.

Such efforts on the national forest often were performed by one or more Forest Service staff specialists, including a botanist, two wildlife biologists, and two ecosystems technicians. These officials performed systematic, targeted surveys to discover rare species on national forest land. For example, after a citizen reported seeing a rare species of clover near national forest land one summer, Wayne National Forest officials conducted a survey the following spring in an effort to determine whether the plant was growing on national forest land, so they could take measures to protect it. Recent monitoring surveys have focused on hawk and snake species. In fiscal year 1995, federal forest officials spent more than $20,000 on threatened, endangered, and sensitive species work.

Although state officials in Ohio consulted a rare species database managed by another state agency before starting major management activities, proactive species identification and protection efforts were limited. As one Ohio state forest official explained, "We check timber sales areas in the rare species database [maintained by another state agency], but we don't go looking for species, and we don't inventory every acre." One state official did describe an unusual effort: a clearcut made to promote small mammals near the den of a rare rattlesnake species. Overall, however, state officials were less likely than federal officials to undertake extensive efforts solely for the purpose of identifying or protecting rare species. The state did not track expenditures related to rare species.

Indiana

In Indiana, as in Ohio, federal officials performed more activities to identify and protect rare species than did state officials. In fiscal year 1995, Hoosier National Forest officials spent $22,904 on threatened, sensitive, and endangered species work. They completed several projects, including permanent plot monitoring of a plant on the forest "species of concern" list. When officials discovered bald eagles—a federally listed species under the Endangered Species Act—on the forest, they closed access to a trail near the roosting site and began to monitor the area to keep people away. More broadly, federal officials performed systematic inventories on more than 15,000 acres to learn more about stream and terrestrial habitat for rare species.

State officials devoted lower levels of effort to rare species projects. They did regularly check a rare species database, provided by another agency, to see if a particular species was in the vicinity of a planned management activity. On one state forest, a forest official tracked rare species discovered on the forest for addition to the natural preserves database. This individual's rare species work was only part time, however; his primary responsibilities involved timber management. Moreover, most state forest officials' rare species work was cooperative rather than leading. For example, on one state forest,

The [nature preserves agency] did a review of the property over the last two years, and they found a few areas they recommended we either classify as nature preserve or change management—no timber or wildlife enhancement—due to special habitat and the existence of rare species. We have had a couple of meetings with that agency to discuss this recommendation.

It is important to note that such rare species work by a different state agency does not indicate a level of rare species work on state forests as high as that on the national forest. In addition to the higher amount of work that federal officials do directly, they also may gain assistance from outside agencies such as the U.S. Fish and Wildlife Service with regard to rare species. With federal forest agency botanists and biologists on staff, more projects relating to rare species identification and protection occur on the national than on state forests.

Washington and Oregon

In both Pacific Northwest forest pairs, federal officials undertook more rare species identification and protection work than did state officials. Prior to fiscal year 1995, federal officials on Gifford Pinchot National Forest and Siuslaw National Forest performed substantial rare species survey and research work to revise zoning in forest plans to expand protection for rare species such as the northern spotted owl. In fact, the 1990 U.S. Fish and Wildlife Service listing of the northern spotted owl as endangered throughout its range created significant constraints for federal and state officials alike. Across both agencies in both Pacific Northwest forest pairs, officials were required to avoid harming these species—a requirement that posed a potentially large threat to timber harvesting activities on the forests. As timber sale quantities on national forests in the Pacific Northwest fell dramatically, President Clinton convened a "forest summit" in Portland, Oregon, to lay the groundwork for revised national forest plans, which subsequently expanded protection for the northern spotted owl and other rare species such as the marbled murrelet (which was listed as a threatened species under the Endangered Species Act).

Following significant zoning changes and restrictions on where timber could be sold, prior to fiscal year 1995 federal officials in Washington and Oregon reduced the level of resources devoted to identifying and protecting the northern spotted owl in 1995. They continued to perform work related to rare species beyond those listed by the U.S. Fish and Wildlife Service, however, illustrating their proactive efforts in rare species identification and protection.

Beyond listed species work, in fiscal year 1995 federal officials in Washington completed projects related to wolves, amphibians, reptiles, birds, and mollusks. Gifford Pinchot National Forest officials surveyed close to 50,000 acres of national forest to learn more about gray wolf movements, as an aid in possible future recovery efforts of this rare species. In addition, federal officials completed amphibian and reptile surveys at 126 sites, where researchers gathered information about species, habitat, and behavior. Scientists conducted goshawk surveys on 5,000 acres to develop guidelines for management practices that might be beneficial to these birds, whose population is low. In addition, officials focused on three rare mollusk species, conducting a survey that resulted in a timber sale modification to leave big leaf maples that provide habitat for the mollusks. The federal agency spent about $135,000 for threatened and endangered species work. It spent an additional $74,000 for wildlife, some of which contributed to projects related to rare species.

State officials in Washington devoted substantial resources to identify and protect rare species that were likely to affect timber harvesting. As a response to Endangered Species Act listings, survey crews specializing in northern spotted owl and marbled murrelet species completed surveys aimed at avoiding undue risk prior to timber sales. In fact, state officials spent more than $7 million on threatened and endangered species surveys linked to timber harvest. State officials performed little work proactively, however, to identify or protect rare species that were not likely to constrain the state agency's ability to sell timber.

In Oregon, federal officials exhibited greater efforts toward rare species identification and protection than did state officials. As described above, prior to fiscal year 1995 federal officials had performed substantial amounts of research and monitoring to create a land management plan to provide greater protection for rare species such as the northern spotted owl. Thus, by fiscal year 1995 fewer resources were being spent for the owl and the marbled murrelet than state officials in Oregon were spending (described below). In fiscal year 1995, however, federal officials undertook numerous projects to identify and protect other rare species. Accomplishments included rare species habitat inventory on 10,000 acres of terrestrial and 72 miles of stream habitat. Federal officials built eighty-one rare species structures, including snags for cavity-nesting birds and enclosures around snowy plover nesting pairs to keep out people and predators. They also performed rare species terrestrial habitat enhancement, such as increasing preferred vegetation for a rare butterfly species, on fifteen acres. Federal officials spent more than $224,000 on threatened, endangered, and sensitive species and another $240,000 on wildlife, some of which was for projects related to rare species.

Like their counterparts in Washington, state officials in Oregon devoted substantial resources in fiscal year 1995 to identifying two rare species—the northern spotted owl and the marbled murrelet—that were subject to Endangered Species Act restrictions. Before completing a timber sale, the state was required to demonstrate to the U.S. Fish and Wildlife Service that no northern spotted owls or marbled murrelets would be harmed. This demonstration was achieved by performing survey activities, research, and habitat classification. In fiscal year 1995, the state agency spent more than $1.6 million on such activities.

The state's rare species work was limited predominantly to efforts required to sell timber, however. Outside of timber sale concerns, state forest officials undertook little rare species work. As one state official explained, "For other rare species, we haven't found efficient methods and protocols, so we have not focused efforts on identification or protection."

Summary

Overall, analysis of projects and resources devoted to identifying and protecting rare species indicates important differences by level of government. In each forest pair, greater efforts to identify and protect rare species occurred on the national forest than on the state forests.

In the Pacific Northwest, where rare species have had the most impact on forest activities (via the Endangered Species Act), the state agencies did provide greater identification and protection work than did the federal agencies. The federal agencies had already devoted considerable resources to protection for these species prior to fiscal year 1995, however, establishing more restricted areas where timber harvesting would not be permitted. The state agencies devoted much less effort to proactively identifying and protecting rare species that did not affect their ability to sell timber. Thus, federal officials across the four forest pairs completed more proactive work to identify and protect rare species than did state officials.

Ecosystem Research and Monitoring

In addition to identification of rare and threatened species, research and monitoring can be devoted to learning more about the broader forest ecosystem. Such activities occur outside the timber planning and sale process. In other words, the primary goal of such efforts is not to mitigate timber harvesting damage but to generate information to be used in developing protection projects or to be factored into long-term decision making. Lee (1993) and other scholars advocate close monitoring to learn about the effects of human actions on the environment. My analysis across these forest pairs indicates that federal officials devote greater efforts to ecosystem research and monitoring than do state officials.

In Ohio, federal agency officials devoted considerable effort to ecosystem research and monitoring. In fiscal year 1995, officials spent $545,810 on such efforts. These expenditures covered the costs of data gathering, inventorying, and monitoring outside the scope of particular timber sales. For example, this line item partially funded opportunity area analysis research. Another effort involved inventorying an aquatic ecosystem related to a creek. The most significant ecosystem research project involved ecological classification efforts, which help agency officials better understand different ecosystems for future planning.

In contrast, state agency officials in Ohio devoted little effort to such ecosystem research and monitoring. As one Ohio state forest official explained, "We don't do much ecosystem monitoring; just the cruise that focuses on overstory." The only ecosystem research that state officials performed in fiscal year 1995 was a pilot study, based on U.S. Environmental Protection Agency (EPA) guidelines and using federal grant funds, that involved test plots to measure soil conditions, topography, vegetation, and other ecosystem components. One official predicted that such research would not be continued, however, because "monitoring [the whole forest community] is time-consuming and doesn't provide commercial timber information that we need."

In Indiana, federal officials undertook numerous ecosystem research and monitoring activities in fiscal year 1995. For example, Hoosier National Forest officials completed research and analyses focusing on soil erosion and exotic species introductions. Federal officials inventoried about twenty-five miles of streams and thirty-one miles of lakeshore. Aquatic, riparian, and terrestrial inventory work involved botanists and biologists seeking an overall understanding of major vegetative communities, as well as special features, in different areas. In fiscal year 1995, federal officials spent $547,766 on ecosystem monitoring and research efforts.

On the other hand, state forest officials in Indiana devoted fewer resources to ecosystem research and monitoring. Traditionally, monitoring and inventorying work on Indiana state forests has emphasized timber resources, with nontimber resource data collection primarily a by-product of examining trees. As one state official noted, "We're limited by manpower as to what we can monitor, even as we are increasingly recognizing how important the different resources are besides just trees for timber."

In Washington, federal officials undertook substantial ecosystem research and monitoring efforts in fiscal year 1995. Such efforts included comprehensive watershed analyses to determine watershed health, identify needed restoration projects, and define monitoring needs. In fiscal year 1995, federal officials spent more than $1.7 million on ecosystem research and monitoring work.

Compared to federal officials, state officials in Washington performed less ecosystem research and monitoring. One Washington state forest official explained, "Our focus for forest health is timber. The trust mandate requires management for present and future beneficiaries; if we put more resources into nontimber benefits, we might face lawsuits for mismanagement of the trust." Other state officials described a shift toward broader monitoring efforts. For example, one state official said, "The traditional inventory focused on trees and timber. But the new inventory designed to qualify for a HCP [Habitat Conservation Plan] with the U.S. Fish and Wildlife Service will include wildlife, dead trees, shrubs, herbs, etc."

In Oregon, federal officials completed numerous projects related to ecosystem research and monitoring in fiscal year 1995. In addition to forest planning, Siuslaw National Forest officials completed several watershed analyses, focusing on many aspects of the forest ecosystem. They undertook studies focusing on ecological impacts of fire and on plant associations linked to specific types of sites. In fiscal year 1995, federal officials spent more than $1.3 million on ecosystem research and monitoring efforts.

On the state forests in Oregon, officials did not place such a high emphasis on ecosystem research and monitoring work. One state official said, "Other than owl and murrelet surveys, we do not generally do systematic surveys for nontimber resources on state forests. If we tried to do more comprehensive surveys, the counties would be upset that we're spending resources in this way."

The state forest agency has contracted out aquatic surveys to another state agency. In fiscal year 1995, aquatic habitat surveys were completed for about 100 miles of streams. One reason for these aquatic inventories was to provide information about a rare species of salmon that may become listed under the Endangered Species Act (ESA). Another reason was to support the state agency's HCP, which allows continued timber sales in areas where ESA-listed species may be present. Also in support of the HCP, the state was developing a new inventory system that would include items such as nontree vegetation, cultural sites, and special forest products. Thus, the state agency was moving toward broader inventories, in support of ecosystem research and monitoring efforts rather than focusing on trees only. Nevertheless, in fiscal year 1995, state officials performed lower levels of ecosystem research and monitoring than did federal officials.

Overall, analysis indicates systematic differences in officials' efforts devoted to ecosystem research and monitoring. In each forest pair, federal efforts by forest agency officials included more work focusing on these nontimber projects than did state efforts.

Soil and Watershed Protection and Improvement

Soils and watersheds are critical forest ecosystem components. Activities to protect them include minimization of harm during management activities and improvement work to repair existing damage. Data indicate that although officials in state and federal agencies undertook similar levels of efforts to minimize harm, federal agency officials performed more improvement activities.

Protection during Timber Harvesting

Timber harvesting has long been known to have the potential to cause increased water runoff, which can lead to soil erosion and stream siltation. Because agency officials typically contract harvesting operations with private parties, officials' efforts to minimize soil and watershed damage take the form of restrictions on contractors and monitoring for contract compliance. Contract restrictions and compliance monitoring efforts to protect soils and watersheds are similar across levels of governance.

Ohio State Forests   In Ohio, efforts to protect soil and watershed on Ohio state forests from timber harvesting damage center on "best management practices" (BMPs) for erosion control. At the time of contract signing, state officials hold a presale meeting with the contractor to discuss BMPs stipulated in the contract. BMPs are especially important for the use and maintenance of the road system, where most of the soil erosion occurs. Agency officials follow a set of BMP guidelines in laying out haul and skid roads, including keeping haul road grades less than 10 percent and skid road grades less than 20 percent, following contours along hillsides, and constructing sediment barriers at the base of slopes. Stream crossings are to be at right angles to the stream, using culverts or bridges, and no cutting is to be done within twenty-five feet of a stream bank. During periods of inactivity, all active roads are to be graded and water bars installed.

BMPs include seasonal restrictions. Logging on state forests generally takes place only between April 1 and December 1, to reduce damage from cutting in wet weather conditions that exacerbate erosion problems. The timber sale administrator may suspend operations during this period, however, if weather conditions are likely to lead to erosion problems, and he or she may allow operations outside the normal logging period if weather conditions allow.

After completing cutting on an Ohio state forest, the contractor must immediately clear and smooth skid trails, logging roads, and loading areas and construct water diversions on the trails and roads. Usually the contractor also must supply and apply lime, fertilizer, seed, and mulch in specified quantities on all skid trails, haul roads, and decking areas to promote vegetative growth. To ensure contractor completion of contract requirements, the state requires a performance bond—typically 25 percent of the value of the highest-valued cutting section.

BMPs are of no value unless they are followed. To monitor compliance, the state timber sale administrator spends time in the forest observing cutting operations. One state official estimated that he monitors loggers for a half day at the beginning of the operation, then visits them at least three times per week, for an hour or two per visit. He explained, "During these visits I look for damage, such as skidder trails ripping up the ground, damage to other trees, inappropriate stream crossings, or skidder tracks that stray from the skidder trails." On the loggers' last day at a cutting section, the state timber administrator typically spends the whole day with the loggers, to ensure that they fulfill the BMP requirements for items such as cleaning up stumps and building water bars to reduce erosion.

Wayne National Forest   On the national forest in Ohio, contractors face restrictions similar to those on the state forests. Contracts typically include thirty or more clauses specifying practices to protect soils and watersheds. For example, loggers must install water bars when they cease operations. Agency officials follow certain procedures in laying out the sale, including designating roads away from steep slopes, unstable soil, and stream banks. As with the state agency, federal agency timber contracts generally allow harvesting only between April 1 and

December 1, although the timber sale administrator can make exceptions on the basis of weather and soil conditions. Contractors also are required to prepare, seed, and mulch all constructed skid roads, using specified seed mixtures and quantities.

A federal official serving as timber sale administrator monitors contractor compliance on Wayne National Forest. The contractor files an operating plan to indicate intended days of operation, so the federal official can plan visits and inspections. The administrator typically spends a half day with an operator, one to four times each week, depending on the contractor's reputation. Like state officials, federal officials can use the performance bond (10 percent of the value of the entire timber sale) as a remedy, to encourage compliance with soil and watershed protection requirements.

To corroborate the finding that there is no significant difference between timber sale contractual requirements to protect soils and watersheds, I spoke with a logger who had participated in timber sales on both forests. He reported that, based on his experience, there was no substantial difference in stringency to protect soils and watersheds across the agencies.

Indiana State Forests   In Indiana, harvest contracts for Indiana state forests and Hoosier National Forest require similar levels of soil and watershed protection. At the state level, standard logging contracts require contractors to mitigate damage:

> The Purchaser must take whatever precautions are necessary, at the sole discretion of the Seller, to prevent soil erosion, water pollution, or other conditions detrimental to the environment on State or adjacent private lands. The Purchaser shall prevent rutting of skid trails, haul roads, and log yards. The Purchaser shall abandon all skid trails, haul roads and log yards in accordance with "Logging Roads and Skid Trails" specifications and/or at the discretion of the Seller.

The "Logging Roads and Skid Trails" document specifies creation of water breaks to reduce erosion, including diagrams and standards for water break construction, log landing area runoff, and bridges and culverts.

Contractors also must adhere to a checklist of erosion control items, including creating skid trails on grades of less than 10 percent, providing for good drainage on trails and roads, and diverting water flow into protected areas. After logging is complete, they must smooth roads and trails, remove any logging slash from streams, seed certain areas to encourage vegetation, and put gravel on sensitive road areas.

To monitor compliance with such requirements, state timber sale administrators visit logging sites at least weekly. As one state official described,

> We're required to visit logging jobs once per week, but we usually go out more often to monitor. If I go out on the first day and see something that disturbs me, if the crew is inexperienced, or if I haven't worked with them yet, then I may visit once a day, and if there are problems I might stay all day to monitor. With a good crew I may visit a couple of times per week, for a few hours at a time.

Enforcement of contractor requirements is facilitated by a performance deposit. The contractor must submit 5 percent of the timber sale bid amount as a deposit. If the contractor creates excessive damage without mitigation, the state timber sale administrator can recommend withholding the deposit. This threat is new; the performance deposit requirement began just a few years ago. One state official said that he did not recall ever withholding any portion of any deposit because contractors usually reach an acceptable level of compliance:

> Of course, the perfect job would leave no damage, and the whole area would be cleaned up, but in reality you have to look at "acceptable" instead of "perfect." There's always going to be some understory damage, which is usually acceptable, but we're more concerned about overstory damage or harming rare species.

Hoosier National Forest   On the national forest in Indiana, contractors are required to follow numerous practices to minimize damage to soils and watersheds. The operating season typically is restricted to six months—May through October—when less damage is likely to occur, unless the timber sale administrator determines that ground conditions are acceptable for harvesting outside of this period. The standard contract requires stream course protection measures such as preventing debris from entering, building culverts or bridges to provide unobstructed flow, not dragging trees across stream courses, and not using wheeled or tracked equipment in stream courses. It also requires operations to "reasonably minimize soil erosion," including sloping log landing areas and constructing temporary drains. After logging, the contractor must maintain soil erosion control structures until they become stabilized, up to one year after harvesting.

To ensure compliance with such requirements, the timber sale administrator visits logging sites about twice a week, usually for a half day. Similar to contractors on state forests, if contractors on the national forest fail to comply with contract requirements, then federal officials may retain their performance bond.

Washington State Forests   In Washington, loggers on state and national forests face similar requirements for soil and watershed protection. On Washington state forests, contractors must construct water bars across haul roads, skid trails, and fire trails to control soil erosion and water pollution. Timber may not be felled into or dragged across designated streams, and any slash or debris falling into such a stream must be removed so that the natural streambed and bank vegetation will not be damaged. Logging equipment may not operate within a riparian management zone or "leave tree" (trees left standing) area. Skid road locations must be approved by the contract administrator before timber is cut.

A state official designated as timber sale administrator monitors contract compliance. This official visits logging sites to ensure that loggers are following contractual conditions. In the past, staff reductions led to low levels of on-site compliance monitoring. An audit of the agency's timber harvest management in the early 1990s revealed deficiencies in monitoring. Thus, monitoring efforts were stepped up in fiscal year 1995 to a minimum of one site visit per week during timber harvest operations. A typical visit lasts a half day. Performance security for large sales (with a value of $1 million or more) usually is set at $100,000, but the security is rarely, if ever, withheld.

Gifford Pinchot National Forest   Loggers working on Gifford Pinchot National Forest in Washington also face numerous requirements to protect soil and watershed during timber harvesting. For example, no debris may be left in stream courses, nor may timber be dragged across them. Culverts must be built where necessary to prevent harmful runoff. Log landings must be ditched or sloped to prevent erosion. Where erosion control structures are needed, the contractor must build them and maintain them until the ground is stabilized, up to one year after harvest completion. After harvesting is done, the contractor must apply seed, fertilizer, and mulch as specified and scarify designated landings, roads, and skid trails. Moreover, the timing of timber harvest operations usually is restricted to protect northern spotted owl nesting and deer and elk winter range and calving areas, as well as during times of wet conditions that might lead to considerable soil damage. The sale administrator can shut down a sale whenever conditions require it to protect resources such as soils and watersheds.

The timber sale administrator visits a logging site periodically to check conditions. If damage occurs, he or she may suspend operations. One administrator estimated that this happens about ten times per year, after which a contractor usually remedies the situation and continues. A performance bond of 10 percent of the sale value is held by the federal agency, in case a contractor fails to meet all contract requirements, including those relating to soil and watershed protection. This money is rarely withheld for damage, however; one experienced administrator reported that in more than ten years on the forest, he's withheld performance money only "a few times."

Oregon State Forests   In Oregon, loggers face similar requirements for soil and watershed protection across levels of governance. Harvest contracts for work on Oregon state forests require high levels of soil and watershed protection. For example, loggers must maintain roads to safeguard soil, water, and drainage structures and ensure that exposed soil will not erode. The contract also limits logging systems to those that minimize soil disturbance, such as requiring the use of preexisting skid roads and trails whenever possible and ceasing operations where soils are rutted or excavated to a depth of twelve inches or more. As described in the contract, the purchaser must "take all necessary precautions to prevent damage to stream banks, any stream course, lake, reservoir, or forested wetland within or adjacent to the timber sale area." The contract also specifies requirements for drainage culverts, as well as seeding and mulching after operations are complete.

To monitor contract compliance, the designated agency timber sale administrator visits the site on the first day of operations, observing for a few hours or up to a whole day. The administrator typically makes subsequent visits once or twice per week. If there are noncompliance items, the administrator may suspend operations until the contractor remedies the problem. One timber sale administrator told me that, of a dozen or so contracts per year on his forest, operations typically are suspended on about two. Once harvesting is complete, the final inspection focuses on items such as water drainage, road grading, and slash treatment. The administrator documents any problems in an inspection report and follows up with a letter, which usually results in an acceptable contractor remedy. At stake is the contractor's performance bond, which is 20 percent of the timber sale value.

Siuslaw National Forest   Timber sales on the national forest in Oregon also are subject to stringent soil and watershed protection requirements. The standard sale contract for harvesting on Siuslaw National Forest is nearly the same as that used by agency personnel on Gifford Pinchot National Forest. Thus, loggers must abide by requirements in treating stream courses, log landings, culverts, erosion control structures, and postharvest seeding.

The timber sale administrator performs contract monitoring on national forest timber operations. The administrator meets with the contractor prior to the start of operations and then typically spends several hours on site the first day, followed by brief visits at least three times per week for the duration of timber harvesting operations. The administrator documents any problems and works with the operators to solve them. If necessary, the administrator may write a "breach letter," warning of a breach in contract, but such a step is rare, occurring in less than 10 percent of the sales. The next step, which is even more rare, would be to withhold a portion of the performance bond. One administrator said that the agency's decreasing sale volume has improved compliance, as the more professional loggers have continued to harvest timber while the less professional "farmers with tractors" have not.

Summary

Across the four forest pairs, federal and state contract restrictions and compliance monitoring to protect soils and watersheds do not differ significantly. Officials at both levels undertake similar efforts to minimize soil and watershed harm during timber operations.

Improvements Outside of Timber Sales

Prevention of soil and watershed degradation during timber operations certainly is an important environmental safeguard that state and federal officials take seriously. Even greater environmental protection of soil and watersheds, however, involves improving conditions outside of timber sales. On this measure, federal officials devote greater efforts than do state officials.

Ohio   In Ohio, federal officials perform more reclamation work than do state officials to reverse soil and watershed harm caused by past activities such as coal mining. In fact, in fiscal year 1995, Wayne National Forest officials spent more than $700,000 on soil improvement work. That year, agency officials treated an eroded portion of a power line corridor—which had been damaged by user-developed off-road vehicle trails—by reforming the slope, constructing water bars, applying seeds, and installing fences to discourage further abuse. Federal officials also stabilized a section of an eroding stream bank and planted seedlings to reforest fifteen acres of riparian area.

At the state level, Ohio officials did not spend substantial amounts of money on reclamation projects. Such activities typically were funded by the state reclamation agency, which is responsible for any reclamation projects on state forests. Ohio state forest officials indicated that, in fiscal year 1995, the reclamation agency performed work on three state forests, primarily to plug abandoned mines and plant trees. Although output quantities were not available for such work, one official indicated that work on one of the three state forests covered fifteen acres of land reclamation.

Indiana   In Indiana, as in Ohio, federal forest agency officials devoted greater effort to soil and watershed improvement activities than did state forest agency officials. A major emphasis on Hoosier National Forest was abandoned road work, which involved building water bars and seeding vegetation to reduce erosion and installing gates and barrier posts to reduce motor vehicle access. Federal officials also performed wetlands restoration projects. In fiscal year 1995, federal officials completed soil and watershed improvement projects on thirty-five acres.

State forest officials in Indiana did not undertake as many soil or watershed improvement projects. Although Indiana state forest officials did work to bring all existing roads up to erosion standards, they did not take on any major projects to reforest open land or improve soil or watersheds in fiscal year 1995.

Washington   In Washington, federal officials performed more soil and watershed improvement activities than did state officials. A major emphasis on Gifford Pinchot National Forest was road restoration and closing, to minimize erosion problems. Other soil and watershed improvements included seeding, tree planting, and erosion control blankets. Across the forest, such improvements were completed on more than 150 acres in fiscal year 1995.

The state agency in Washington was less proactive in performing soil and watershed improvement projects. Instead, such projects were undertaken through programs outside the agency. For example, a "Jobs in the Environment" program makes use of dislocated timber workers to improve watersheds across different forest ownerships, including the state. Program activities on state forest lands in fiscal year 1995 included road stabilization and stream bank protection. Washington state forest officials did not perform or fund substantial levels of restoration work, however.

Oregon   In Oregon, federal officials performed significant soil and watershed improvement efforts. In fiscal year 1995, Siuslaw National Forest officials completed soil and watershed improvement work such as pulling back slide material and scarifying the ground to encourage vegetation on 178 acres. Officials stabilized drainage on 282 miles of road and decommissioned another 30 miles of road to reduce erosion. In addition, officials completed 140 miles of riparian improvement activities, such as planting hardwood and conifer trees to provide natural stream structures, growing herbaceous cover to control erosion, and removing noxious weeds.

Unfortunately, data are not available regarding state agency soil and watershed improvement activities in Oregon. Work is undertaken at the forest unit level, often mixed with other forest management activities, so data are not available to specify activities across Oregon state forests for the fiscal year. The fact that officials do not track these activities statewide may be an indication that they do not receive high levels of attention. Without such data, however, no comparison can be made with federal officials' efforts in Oregon.

Conclusion

In evaluating relative levels of effort by federal and state officials regarding environmental protection, it is necessary to examine multiple indicators. Analysis of four such indicators reveals that federal forest policies promote environmental protection more than do state forest policies. Across the forest pairs, federal officials consistently exhibit greater levels of ecosystem-level management, rare species identification and protection, ecosystem research and monitoring, and soil and watershed improvement. In just one indicator—mitigation of soil and watershed damage during timber harvesting—federal and state performance is similar.[2]

These results support the argument that different policy performance is likely at different levels of governance in a federal system. This analysis examines public forest policy, but there are many other policy sectors in which decisions are made regarding which outputs to pursue. Often, such decisions involve choices between economic development and other goals such as environmental protection, wealth redistribution, and serving a particular clientele. As this analysis shows, agency officials at higher levels of government are likely to favor goals other than economic development more than are agency officials at lower levels of governance. In contrast, as described in chapter 3, lower-level governments are the more likely locus of policy outputs that favor economic development. Therefore, choices about which level is granted authority for a particular policy area have significant importance in determining the types of outputs likely to be provided.

Although policy outputs are an important measure of policy performance, my analysis does not stop here. For a democracy to function effectively, policymakers must be responsive to citizen demands. In public forest policy (or any other sector), the process of policymaking may be as important—if not more so—than the policy outputs. Thus, analysis should include citizen participation in policy processes. I turn to this topic in chapter 5.

Notes

1. Although tropical forests are among the most diverse and species-rich ecosystems on the planet, temperate forests also contain an incredible abundance of species. For example, in the old-growth forests of the Pacific Northwest, a single tree can provide complex micro-ecologies for more than 1,500 invertebrate species (Kelly and Braasch 1988: 7).

2. This result puts Donald Leal's (1995) study in perspective. Leal argues that in Montana, national forest officials did not provide greater environmental protection than state forest officials. Leal's indicator of environmental protection, however, was the extent to which timber harvesters followed best management practices (BMPs) during harvest operations. As the evidence in this chapter shows, even if protection of soil and watershed during harvesting is similar across agencies, other environmental protection indicators are likely to show that national officials provide higher levels of environmental protection.

5 Federal Agency Strength:
Citizen Participation in Policy Processes

Participation of the governed in their government is, in theory, the cornerstone of democracy—a revered idea that is vigorously applauded by virtually everyone.

—Sherry Arnstein, "A Ladder of Citizen Participation," 1969

U.S. forest management must be given back to trained and experienced foresters; they are best qualified to scientifically manage our most important renewable natural resource.

—William Maxey, "Foresters: Another Endangered Species?" 1996

In a democratic society, an important measure of policy performance is the role that citizens play in policy processes. Although people largely agree that citizens ought to participate in choosing their elected officials, the proper extent of citizen participation in agency decision making is an unsettled question.

Participation often is cited as a critical link between citizens and government, with the potential to improve policy choices, increase equity, and enhance citizens' capacity to involve themselves in self-governance. Examples abound of policies created by government officials, ignoring citizen input, that fail miserably. In natural resource policy, local environmental conditions and community needs can determine the success of a policy.

On the other hand, citizen participation can be expensive and time-consuming. Many taxpayers demand government that is cheaper and more expedient—a goal that is unlikely to be reached through extensive citizen involvement. More troubling to some people is that citizen participation can result in critical technical decisions being made by nonexperts. Many researchers have demonstrated that citizen decision making about environmental risk is woefully inadequate. For example, nuclear power ranks among the most feared energy sources in the United States, but coal-fired plants, which are more readily accepted, pose far greater human health hazards.

Given the potential benefits and costs of citizen participation, the debate over whether we should have more or less of it is not likely to end soon. My aim is not to settle this dispute one way or the other. Instead, I address the question of how citizen participation varies, if at all, by level of government. Whether or not one believes that greater citizen participation is a good thing, knowing if it differs by level of government allows us to make more informed choices about granting authority to higher or lower government jurisdictions in a federal system.

Two related questions lie at the heart of citizen participation in a federal system. First, do agency officials at one level of government promote citizen participation in policy processes more than do officials at a different level of government? Second, are certain types of citizen interests more likely to participate at different levels of government?

Who Promotes Citizen Participation More?

In the United States, the federal government historically has taken the lead in promoting citizen participation in agency policymaking; lower levels of government have been less accommodating. For example, the Administrative Procedure Act (APA) of 1946 established minimum standards for federal administrative agencies' procedures regarding citizen consultation, input, and information dissemination. Lowering the costs (effort required) to participate may encourage a greater number of participants (see Downs 1957). Thus, the use of no-tice-and-comment periods, public meetings, mailing lists, and other tools to solicit public input should lead to greater participation in pol-icymaking. Whereas these tools frequently have been used at the fed-eral level, they may be less prevalent at the state level. In fact, most states did not enact administrative procedures laws until years after the federal APA—and then only after prodding from federal officials through grant requirements.

Research on factors other than the APA is lacking, however, espe-cially at the state level. State bureaucrats may promote citizen partic-ipation even without rules as specific as those federal bureaucrats face in the APA. Besides this law, other rules might apply. After all, the ex-istence of rules is only one variable among many that may affect offi-cials' behavior regarding encouragement and use of public input. Moreover, devolution proponents have rallied around the idea of get-ting the government "closer to the people," with lower levels regarded as providing better opportunities for citizens to make their voices heard.

In this section, I compare state efforts to federal efforts to encour-age citizen participation in public forest policymaking. Officials can undertake a variety of efforts to encourage citizen participation. For this analysis, I asked officials and citizens to indicate the most signifi-cant types of such efforts undertaken. On the basis of these discus-sions, I examine three indicators of citizen participation efforts: pub-lic meetings, working groups, and mailings. My analysis suggests that differences between state and federal agencies vary by indicator, but overall federal agency officials tend to undertake greater efforts to pro-mote citizen participation (see Table 5.1).

Public Meetings

Public meetings are a classic means for agency officials to encourage public participation. In the analysis here, I focus on meetings held by agency officials in 1995 that were attended by citizens. Results indi-cate that federal officials held more public meetings in Ohio, Wash-ington, and Oregon; federal and state officials held similar levels of public meetings in Indiana. In addition, federal agency meetings

Table 5.1. Officials' Efforts to Encourage Citizen Participation, 1995

	Agency with Greater Efforts			
Indicator	Ohio	Indiana	Washington	Oregon
Public meetings	Federal	Equal	Federal	Federal
Working groups	Equal	Equal	Equal	State
Mailings	Federal	Federal	Federal	Federal

tended to provide higher-quality opportunities for citizen participation than did state agency meetings.

Meeting Quantity

In Ohio, federal officials devoted greater effort to encourage citizen participation through public meetings than did state officials. Notably, Wayne National Forest officials conducted a series of quarterly "community of interest" meetings that were open to the public. Approximately thirty to forty people attended these meetings, representing a diversity of interests—including wildlife, environmental protection, horse riding, hunting, off-road vehicle (ORV) riding, private forest ownership, logging, community tax revenue, oil and gas production, and bird watching. Nearly a dozen national forest officials participated in the meetings, including the forest supervisor, district rangers, and most program managers, where they shared information and answered questions. Although several Ohio state forest officials attended these federal agency meetings, the state agency did not hold any meetings for such a large and diverse group of nonagency participants. State officials' meetings for a broad audience were limited to two informal[1] "open houses" in 1995.

In Indiana, neither federal nor state officials held formal public meetings in 1995. Several federal officials described such meetings as having been counterproductive in the past. For example, one official said, "We don't do formal public meetings any more because they're not useful for information sharing; you get people with their set agendas who don't work together." Another federal official said, "We've found that meetings often lead to shouting matches, with polarized viewpoints, and I've seen studies to back this up." Similarly, a state official said, "We avoid general public meetings much, since they can be rancorous and, with some quiet folks, not everyone gets to speak their mind."

Officials in both agencies held informal open houses, however, for public communication. Such open houses were aimed at generating information about public views and concerns involving specific issues or proposed projects. Open houses were held at the rate of three to ten per month on the state forests and approximately four per month on the national forest.

In Washington, federal officials held between six and nine formal public meetings, which addressed controversial issues. In addition, federal officials held less formal open houses and workshops about four times per month, where officials and citizens discussed plans for the forest's "adaptive management area" as well as specific issues such as damage caused by flooding. Some of these gatherings included as many as fifty citizens.

State officials in Washington held fewer public meetings in 1995. At the field level, Washington state forest officials conducted one to two informal meetings per month, where they met with neighbors and other interested individuals about timber sales or recreational conflicts. In addition, during creation of landscape-level plans for a particular forest, state officials sometimes held public meetings.

In Oregon, federal officials hosted a variety of public meetings in 1995. One federal official in the timber program estimated meeting with citizens about once per month to discuss policies and practices. Officials also held nearly fifty public meetings relating to watershed analyses during the year, each involving fifteen to twenty people. Federal officials met with a recreation group once or twice during the year, and they hosted an annual open house focusing on recreation issues. One federal official working at the forest headquarters estimated that, forest wide, officials held between ten and twenty project-oriented public meetings during the year.

State officials in Oregon hosted numerous public meetings in 1995 for long-range planning purposes. In creating a new regional forest plan, Oregon state forest officials planned to hold several dozen public meetings, in different locations. In addition, a comprehensive recreation plan for one state forest, completed over a two-year period, included more than thirty-six meetings with user groups. Other than for long-range planning, however, officials did not hold frequent public meetings to encourage public participation for activities such as timber sales. One state official commented, "Overall, we do little to encourage public input outside of [long-range] planning." This level of effort contrasts with that by federal officials, who undertook considerable effort to hold public meetings during long-range planning and while making decisions about numerous projects.

Meeting Quality

Meaningful citizen participation is measured not only by meeting quantity but by meeting quality. While the data were insufficient to examine closely state and federal public meeting quality across the four forest pairs, interviews with agency personnel suggested that federal officials tend to seek citizen input more proactively in their public meetings.

An example of the qualitative differences in how public meetings are conducted at the federal and state levels is evident in Ohio. In 1995 federal officials on the Ohio national forest held a series of "community of interest" meetings that were open to the public. The officials invited participants who were interested in a diverse array of forest uses to a site away from the forest offices. Each of these meetings had a structured format and agenda; for the first meeting, a professional facilitator encouraged input from all participants in a variety of formats, including small group discussions, meeting-wide discussions, and collaborative, written lists. Federal officials stressed their desire to gather and learn from citizen input. Following each meeting, forest officials sent participants a written list of public comments compiled from the meeting, along with information about the status of current forest management decisions and activities related to these comments.

In contrast, during 1995 state forest personnel held two informal public meetings, at local forest offices. The primary purpose of these meetings was to explain to the public why the agency had made certain forest management decisions. No professional facilitator was used. Instead, officials mingled with participants to discuss issues with one or a few citizens at a time. Participants did not receive compiled lists of comments from the meetings.

Working Groups

Working groups are constituted to provide an agency with citizen input from a stable set of participants, who meet together on a regular basis. Although this arrangement has certain advantages over "one-shot" public meetings, the opportunity for an agency-selected subset of citizens to influence agency decisions at the expense of the broader public has been recognized. At the federal level, the Federal Advisory Committee Act of 1972 (FACA) sets limits on the use of advisory committees. Further limits are set forth in a 1993 Executive Order preventing the formation of new advisory committees without a "compelling consideration" to justify their existence and Office of Management and Budget (OMB) approval. Nevertheless, on occasion federal officials do create working groups for specific planning processes. In 1995 federal and state forest officials facilitated similar levels of working groups in Ohio, Indiana, and Washington; state officials facilitated working groups more extensively in Oregon.

In Ohio, forest officials in both agencies used working groups to a similar extent. On Wayne National Forest, officials established committees of forest users to help in planning. For example, new trail construction decisions were made in consultation with a working group of trail users. At the state level, a forest advisory council, appointed by the governor, included one representative from each of the following interests: forest-based research activities, small private forestland owners, large private forestland owners, pulp/paper industry, other forest industries, soil science, forest recreation, and "the public." The advisory council met quarterly and provided the agency with guidance about priorities, long-term goals, and controversial issues.

In Indiana, officials used working groups to a similar extent in both agencies. On the national forest, agency personnel convened a diverse array of stakeholder interests over the course of a year to provide recommendations for amending the Forest Plan. In addition, Hoosier National Forest officials created task forces to deal with certain issues, such as a project designed to catalogue existing forest openings and decide which to maintain and where, if any, to create new ones. On the state forests, agency personnel created a horse riding task force to advise in planning for horse trails. More generally, a permanent working group met semiannually and advised the state forester about forest issues.

In Washington, neither federal nor state officials substantially supported working groups. On the national forest, the only working group was a Provincial Advisory Committee, which met bimonthly to help officials set management priorities and to review all timber sales. On state forests, the only working group was one appointed to provide recommendations about landscape plans for a particular forest.

In Oregon, officials encouraged public participation through working groups less on the national forest than on state forests. On the national forest, a Provincial Advisory Committee met quarterly to discuss implementation of the forest management plan. Officials also assembled two or three ad hoc groups to focus on specific issues. On the state forests, officials used working groups more extensively. For example, on one state forest, recreational interests were represented on three standing committees: recreation advisory, nonmotorized trail planning, and motorized trail planning. In addition, a "Forum Group" that included diverse interests provided input to long-range forest planning.

Mailings

A mechanism for public participation that does not require face-to-face interaction at a mutual meeting time is mailings. Two types of mailing are of primary interest here: agency newsletters and letters to targeted individuals regarding specific projects. For newsletters, I compare the quantity mailed and the content, and for letters to targeted individuals I analyze the quantity mailed and the range of interests to whom they were sent. In all four forest pairs, federal officials undertook greater efforts to encourage citizen participation through mailings than did state officials.

Ohio

In Ohio, the state and federal agencies maintained mailing lists of people expressing interest in various issues. The biggest mailing list for the Wayne National Forest included more than 900 recipients, 300 of whom received quarterly newsletters in 1995. Ohio state forest officials maintained a mailing list for the agency's quarterly newsletter, which they sent to nearly 5,000 recipients.

Although the state agency had a larger number of mailings, these mailings focused on describing recent agency accomplishments rather than soliciting public input. In contrast, the federal agency newsletter was several times longer, and, in addition to describing accomplishments, it included a substantial list of dozens of proposed actions with information about which officials to contact for input (see Table 5.2). Thus, the federal newsletter was designed to foster public comments more than the state newsletter.

Not only did federal officials encourage citizen input through newsletters more than state officials, but they also fostered input more through letters sent to targeted individuals regarding specific projects. A national forest official indicated that agency personnel sent letters to several people who were likely to be impacted by each agency action. For example, a few dozen times in 1995, four or five parties received letters relating to proposed oil or gas permits. Ohio state forest officials, in contrast, did not send as many letters.

Indiana

In Indiana, federal agency officials sent quarterly newsletters to several hundred recipients. These newsletters provided extensive information about ongoing and planned activities, as well as contact personnel for public input. Indiana state forest officials, on the other hand, did not provide a state forest newsletter.

In addition to providing quarterly newsletters, federal officials in Indiana sent many letters to interested parties when specific projects were planned. These letters went to adjacent landowners as well as to individuals who had expressed interest in a particular issue area. For example, one Hoosier National Forest official described sending at

Table 5.2. Comparison of 1995 Sample Newsletter Contents, Ohio

Agency	Subject	Page Length	Related to Specific Public Forest Project?
State	Welcome	0.5	No
	Fall 1994 fire season	0.5	No
	Tree pruning tips	0.5	No
	Forest ecology general components	1	No
	Pest quarantine	0.5	Yes
	Upcoming events (e.g., county fair)	0.5	Yes
Federal	Message from forest supervisor	0.5	No
	Cemetery restoration	1.5	Yes
	"Community of Interest" meetings	1	No
	Forest fire research	0.5	Yes
	Fishing event	0.5	Yes
	Wetlands monitoring	0.5	Yes
	Forest trail improvement	0.5	Yes
	Lease sale	1	Yes
	"Tree Source" award	1	No
	Wetlands restoration	0.5	Yes
	Creek restoration	1	Yes
	Land acquisition	1	Yes
	Reclamation/rehabilitation	0.5	Yes
	Wildlife habitat improvement	0.5	Yes
	Water quality surveying	0.5	Yes
	Road reconstruction	0.5	Yes
	Community celebrations	1	No
	Firefighter training	0.5	No
	Restoration work	1	Yes
	Water quality monitoring	2	Yes
	Project status and contact names for 51 projects	6	Yes

least one such letter per month, to about fifty or sixty people. Another federal official sent 800 letters to individuals identified as having an interest in a proposal to allow a private organization to build a horse trail on the national forest.

On Indiana state forests, officials reported contacting adjacent landowners before planned timber sales. State officials also contacted groups directly affected by certain proposed activities. For example, one official contacted horse riders to inform them of plans to close a horse camp. Overall, however, state officials did not provide as many mailings, to as many people, as did federal officials.

Washington

In Washington, federal officials mailed a semiannual newsletter to about 400 interested parties. The newsletter, typically forty pages in length, described all projects that were subject to National Environmental Policy Act (NEPA) requirements; it included maps, schedules, and personnel to contact to provide input. State officials, in contrast, did not provide a newsletter. Although the state department of natural resources (of which the forest agency is a part) did print an annual report describing financial and project activities for the previous year, this report did not provide details about future projects, nor did it indicate which officials to contact to provide input.

Federal and state officials in Washington sent letters to interested publics about upcoming projects such as timber sales. In 1995, Gifford Pinchot National Forest officials sent letters to about 120 recipients for each timber sale and other projects (e.g., trail building, campsite work, rare species protection) for which they had completed environmental assessments. Similarly, Washington state forest officials sent letters to interested parties for activities for which they had completed environmental checklists. One state official estimated that the agency sent more than twenty such letters per month in 1995, each to about a dozen recipients. State letters were related to a narrower range of projects, however; more than 85 percent of the letters in one four-month period were for timber sales, with few letters related to other projects.

Oregon

In Oregon, federal officials provided a quarterly newsletter to about 1,300 recipients, highlighting proposed actions for which there was opportunity for public input. Oregon state forest officials also produced a newsletter (bimonthly), which they sent to about 2,000 recipients. Unlike the federal agency's newsletter, this publication was designed more as a tool for sharing the agency's accomplishments than for encouraging public input regarding specific projects. In addition, state officials kept a mailing list of approximately 800 requesters who received a quarterly newsletter featuring updates on the long-range forest planning process. They also sent a recreational newsletter to about 400 recipients. Although these recreational and planning newsletters encouraged citizen involvement in planning processes, they generally did not provide information to encourage citizen participation in specific agency decisions.

In addition to newsletters, officials in Oregon sent targeted letters related to specific projects. Siuslaw National Forest officials sent targeted letters to solicit citizen participation in agency decisions more than did state officials. For example, one federal official with recreational program responsibilities estimated sending about seventy-five different letters during the year, each going to an average of thirty people interested in specific recreational use decisions. Federal officials also sent letters relating to any project for which an environmental assessment was performed, such as timber sales, land exchanges, right-of-way grants, and special use permits. Meanwhile, Oregon state forest officials sent notification letters to a more narrow set of citizens—those interested in timber production. Moreover, most recipients of timber harvesting notifications were not parties seeking to provide input into agency decision making but timber consultants prospecting for business with the timber purchasers. Thus, in Oregon, as in the other forest pairs, federal officials used newsletters and targeted letters to encourage citizen participation in agency decision making for specific projects more than did state officials.

Which Types of Citizens Participate?

The second fundamental question about citizen participation in a federal system focuses on the interests of citizens participating at different levels of government. In natural resource policy, a critical distinction is between citizens favoring commodity production and those favoring environmental protection. Although these goals are not necessarily mutually exclusive, in practice the policy demands of citizens with these interests often compete against one another. Researchers have described commodity and preservation interests as participating differently at different levels of government.

Commodity interests favor active management of forests for marketable products, such as timber. Commodity forest uses tend to be among the higher-impact activities, with a substantial potential to alter forest conditions.

Several researchers have argued that people who favor commodity forest uses are more active at lower levels of government. Sabatier (1974), using Schattschneider's "scope of conflict" model,[2] suggests that commodity interests advocate lower-level government authority, where they will find regulators who are more attuned to promoting economic development. This preference is evident in western commodity users' support for the "sagebrush rebellion" in the late 1970s and early 1980s, when calls for devolution of federal lands to the state level were fueled by the desire to produce greater quantities of commodities.

Although the term "preservationist" has been used by opponents as a negative label for people who favor minimization of forest management activities, the term "preservation interests" is an appropriate descriptor for the preferences of some citizens. Preservation as a forest "use" refers to activities (or lack thereof) directed at protecting the forest community from human actions that have potential to damage the forest. Compared to timber uses, preservation uses tend to be among the lowest-impact activities, with significantly reduced potential to alter forest conditions.

A key set of citizens favoring preservation is environmental advocacy groups. The growth in membership and resources of these groups over the past two decades signals an increase in active participation among preservation interests. Such growth has been especially important at the federal level. Membership in the five largest national environmental organizations—the National Wildlife Federation, the National Audubon Society, the Sierra Club, the Nature Conservancy, and the Wilderness Society—more than doubled during the 1980s (Hendee and Pitstick 1994: 26).

Scholars have described nonbusiness interest groups as more likely to act at the federal level. Peterson (1981) explains that this occurs because the more important policy decisions are made at the federal level and because these interest groups realize they are unlikely to succeed at pressuring local governments to adopt policies that may hurt economic development. Hence, it is likely that environmental groups more actively participate in forest policy at the federal than state level.

To test these theories of participation differences in public forest policy, I interviewed several agency officials and citizens for each forest. These respondents described substantial differences in patterns of participation by interest type. State officials interact more with citizens who have primarily timber interests, whereas federal officials interact more with citizens who have preservation interests.

Agency Officials' Perceptions

In talking with state and federal agency officials with general forest management responsibility, I asked them to rank the amount of communication they had with various citizen participants.[3] Although federal and state officials engaged in communication with a variety of interests, this analysis compares only preservation and timber interests. A substantially higher number of federal officials communicated more with preservation interests than with timber interests. In contrast, a somewhat higher number of state officials communicated more with timber interests than with preservation interests (see Table 5.3).

In Indiana, all four Hoosier National Forest officials said that they communicate most with preservation interests; none reported communicating most with timber interests. Among two Indiana state forest officials, one reported communicating most with timber interests; the other reported most communication with preservation interests.

In Washington, all five Gifford Pinchot National Forest officials said that they communicate most with preservation interests; none reported communicating most with timber interests. Among two Washington state forest officials, one reported communicating most with timber interests; the other reported communicating most with preservation interests.

Table 5.3. Officials' Descriptions of Communications with Citizens

| Agency | *No. of Officials Indicating That They Communicate Most with the Following Interests* | | |
	Total	*Timber*	*Preservation*
Indiana			
Federal	4	0	4
State	2	1	1
Washington			
Federal	5	0	5
State	2	1	1
Oregon			
Federal	6	2	4
State	9	8	1
Total, Federal	15	2	13
Total, State	13	10	3

In Oregon, four of six Siuslaw National Forest officials said that they communicate most with preservation interests; two said that they communicate most with timber interests. Among Oregon state forest officials, eight of nine said that they communicate most with timber interests; one reported communicating most with preservation interests.

Combining responses across the three pairs, thirteen of fifteen federal officials indicated most frequent contact with preservation interests; only two federal officials indicated most frequent contact with timber interests. In contrast, just three of thirteen state officials indicated most frequent contact with preservation interests; ten state officials indicated most frequent contact with timber interests. In other words, it seems that citizens who favor timber are in closer contact with state agency officials, whereas those who favor preservation are in closer contact with federal agency officials.

Citizens' Perceptions

Of course, communication is not a one-way street. To understand communication from citizens' perspectives, I spoke with citizens who participate in forest policymaking. For each of the forest pairs, I chose

Table 5.4. Citizen Participants' Reported Communications with Forest Officials

Citizen Interest Type	No. of Participants Who Communicate More with the Following Agency Officials			
	Total	Federal	State	Equal
Ohio				
Preservation	5	4	0	1
Timber	4	1	3	0
Indiana				
Preservation	8	3	4	1
Timber	5	0	5	0
Washington				
Preservation	6	4	2	0
Timber	5	0	4	1
Oregon				
Preservation	4	4	0	0
Timber	4	1	3	0
Total, Preservation	23	15	6	2
Total, Timber	18	2	15	1

a mix of active citizens favoring either timber or preservation. Their descriptions corroborate the patterns indicated by officials' responses. In all four forest pairs, citizens with timber interests reported more communication with state officials than with federal officials. Conversely, in three of the four pairs, citizens with preservation interests reported more communication with federal officials than with state officials (see Table 5.4).

In Ohio, most people who favor preservation indicated greater communication with federal officials. Four of five citizens favoring preservation said that they have more communication with federal than state agency officials; one such individual indicated equivalent levels of communication across the agencies. In contrast, three of four citizens favoring timber reported higher communication levels with Ohio state forest officials than with Wayne National Forest officials.

In Indiana, unlike in Ohio, citizens favoring preservation described somewhat more communication with state officials than with federal officials. Three of eight participants favoring preservation indicated greater communication with Hoosier National Forest officials, compared to four of eight who reported greater communication with Indiana state forest officials and one who cited equal communication levels. All five individuals favoring timber reported more communication with state officials than with federal officials.

In Washington, four of six individuals favoring preservation reported more communication with federal officials, whereas two reported more communication with state officials. On the other hand, those favoring timber reported more communications with state officials. Four of five timber proponents said that they have more communication with state officials; one reported similar levels with federal and state officials.

In Oregon, all four citizens favoring preservation reported more communication with federal officials than with state officials. In contrast, three of four individuals favoring timber reported more communication with state officials than with federal officials.

Conclusion

To fully evaluate policy performance in a democratic society, we must consider the role of the citizen in policy processes. In the context of federalism, a crucial question about policy processes centers on differences in participation across levels of government.

In talking with agency officials and involved citizens, I discovered that level of government does matter on this measure. Federal officials devote somewhat higher levels of effort to encourage participation, through mailings and public meetings, than do state officials. Moreover, patterns of communication are evident by citizen interest type; officials and citizen participants indicate that federal officials engage in more communication with preservation interests than do state officials. State officials, in contrast, engage in more communication with timber interests than do federal officials.

These results reinforce the notion that, in thinking about the extent of citizen involvement in bureaucracies within a federal system, it is important not to view "government" as a single entity. Differences exist among levels of governance. Thus, decisions about the level in which to place policy authority have important consequences for citizen participation in policy processes. In some sense, one might argue that a federal system provides something for everyone: Preservation proponents can participate more in federal forest policy, and timber advocates can participate more in state forest policy. For people who believe in limited citizen involvement in agency policymaking, state forests are a better example. On the other hand, those who favor more extensive citizen involvement might find that national forests provide a more suitable model.

Notes

1. Officials differentiate between formal and informal meetings on the basis of several factors. Formal meetings tend to have a structured format, an agenda, and discussions among all participants together. Informal meetings feature individual officials who mingle and discuss issues with a few people at a time, without extended discussions among all participants together.

2. Schattschneider (1960) argues that a central political strategy is adjusting the "scope of conflict" to include more or fewer players until the majority of the players favor a particular position. Thus, an issue can be interpreted by interested players as national or local, to be decided at a higher or lower level of government.

3. Unfortunately, officials in Ohio were not asked to do this.

Part Three

Explaining Bureaucratic Behavior in a Federal System

6 Laws and Forest Plans

In the preceding chapters, I compare the performance of state and federal public forest policy. I describe differences in timber sales, profitability, revenue sharing, and environmental protection outputs, along with citizen participation processes. The task now is to explain why these differences exist.

Recall from chapter 1 that our theoretical starting point is the functional theory of federalism. This theory predicts differences in the pursuit of economic versus noneconomic policy goals at different levels in a federal system. Its explanatory power rests on the electoral mechanism, with state and local elected officials facing defeat if they fail to pursue economic development. In agency policymaking, however, electoral selection is replaced by civil service systems; most agency personnel are hired on merit. To understand agency policymaking, we turn to insights from bureaucratic behavior theory.

Bureaucratic behavior theory emphasizes four dominant factors that explain policymaking by agency officials: rules, citizen pressure, agency officials' beliefs, and agency community. Prior research has focused on federal-level agency policymaking. Less is known about whether there are substantive differences in these factors at the state level. For this research, I collected data to make such a comparison across the four forest pairs. I address the first factor—rules—in two chapters: This chapter covers legal and forest plan rules, and chapter 7 examines budget rules. Chapter 8 discusses the remaining three bureaucratic behavior theory factors: citizen pressure, agency officials' beliefs, and agency community.

Rules

Many scholars have examined the role of rules in shaping bureaucratic behavior. Rules define which actions are required, prohibited, or permitted and the sanctions prescribed for transgressions (Ostrom, Gardner, and Walker 1994: 38). Rules are authoritative statements that direct agency officials to behave in certain ways. Agency officials are assumed to respond to external rewards and sanctions, adjusting their behavior to increase the probability of receiving the former and to reduce the likelihood of being subjected to the latter. Elected officials may influence bureaucrats by creating several types of rules, including laws, forest plans, and budget incentives. I discuss the first two types below; the latter type is the subject of chapter 7.

Laws

In societies governed by rule of law, such as the United States, legal statutes are critical for increasing bureaucratic responsiveness. Elected officials often create laws to constrain bureaucratic discretion and prevent changes in the future from elected officials with opposing views (Moe 1989). Many scholars regard laws as a critical determinant of bureaucratic behavior (Weber 1968 [1947]; Clarke and McCool 1985; Ringquist 1990). In environmental policy over the past three decades, statutes have become increasingly specific, and citizens have gained new legal rights of participation. This combination has greatly affected federal agency decisions about environmental regulations (Hoberg 1992).

Legal constraints provide a means to extend the functional theory of federalism to bureaucrats. According to the functional theory, elected officials at different levels of governance create different rules to constrain bureaucrats. Specifically, legal constraints are expected to foster greater economic development at lower levels of governance and greater pursuit of noneconomic goals at higher levels.

In fact, at the federal level, public forest management is subject to National Environmental Policy Act (NEPA) environmental assessment requirements, National Forest Management Act (NFMA) planning mandates, and public participation procedures, among other requirements. Such statutes require federal agency officials to emphasize policymaking that is not necessarily economically efficient and may not promote economic development. In contrast, several states have legislation that emphasizes different policy performance, such as requirements to manage forests for the primary purpose of earning financial returns that are earmarked to fund schools (Souder and Fairfax 1996). In this analysis, I examine whether state and federal forest agencies face different substantive legal constraints and how such differences affect policy performance.

To clarify legal constraints affecting public forest policy, I focus on two kinds of statutory requirements: planning process requirements and limits on forest activities on the ground. Comparisons reveal that federal officials face more constraints than do their state counterparts and that the substantive nature of the constraints is to foster greater environmental protection at the federal level and greater economic development at the state level.

Planning Process Requirements

One important category of legal requirements that constrain officials' behavior involves planning processes. Analysis of planning process requirements reveals that federal forest officials face more constraints than do state forest officials on how they go about planning forest management activities.[1] The most important planning process constraints affecting federal forest officials come from the NFMA and NEPA, which require comprehensive planning and extensive public involvement.

The NFMA and its implementing regulations require the creation of a "Land and Resource Management Plan" ("the Plan") for each national forest every ten years. The statute directs planners to "provide opportunity for public involvement" and to "consult with other interested governmental departments and agencies" in creating the Plan

(16 USCA 1601c). It provides significant detail regarding public input standards:

> [The agency must encourage] public participation in the development, review, and revision of land management plans including, but not limited to, making the plans or revisions available to the public at least three months before final adoption, during which period the Secretary shall publicize and hold public meetings or comparable processes at locations that foster public participation in the review of such plans or revisions (16 USCA 1604d).

Moreover, the NFMA requires the creation of implementing regulations that

> establish procedures, including public hearings where appropriate, to give the Federal, State, and local governments and the public adequate notice and an opportunity to comment on the formulation of standards, criteria, and guidelines applicable to Forest Service Programs (16 USCA 1612a).

In fact, federal officials send a copy of the Plan, free of charge, to anyone requesting it.

In addition to procedural requirements for public involvement, the NFMA and its implementing regulations specify criteria to be included in Plan formulation. For example, planning must include consideration of a broad range of alternative levels of forest outputs. Officials must calculate the financial impacts, including net present value estimates, of suggested alternatives. Furthermore, they must designate land-use zones, called "management areas," within the forest to focus on different management activities.

This latter requirement often leads to conflicts in national forest planning. For example, one official on Wayne National Forest (in Ohio) commented that NFMA public input and management area requirements move the fight over zoning into the public arena, where many participants can and do become involved. In addition, several participants involved in the original planning process for Wayne National Forest recalled that substantial zoning conflicts arose at that time and had yet to be resolved years later.

Unlike federal forest agency officials, those at the state level are not required to adhere to specified planning requirements. In Ohio, an official advisory committee[2] does comment on Ohio state forest policy generally, but it is not intimately involved with planning at the forest level. Instead, agency officials guide the planning process, relying on their expertise to do "what's right for the land" and accommodate existing forest uses. Similarly in Indiana, state forest officials do not face any legal requirements regarding state forest management planning, which has developed internally as administrators seek to formalize existing management practices. Although state officials on Washington state forests are required to provide a public comment period after developing proposed plans, they do not face other legal requirements in creating forest management plans. Finally, for Oregon state forest officials, the lack of specified state forest planning requirements has opened the door to legal challenges under the state administrative procedures law, which prohibits arbitrary decision making in agencies. To prevent future lawsuits, the state forestry board recently had begun developing administrative rules to codify the planning process that state agency personnel should use in the future.

Clearly, federal forest officials face greater planning constraints than do state forest officials. In addition to NFMA planning constraints, federal officials face a second important legal constraint: NEPA requirements. NEPA mandates that any federal agency undertaking "major Federal actions significantly affecting the quality of the human environment" must formally examine alternatives and environmental impacts (42 USCA 4332c). The statute also requires officials to perform "scoping" activities, which include analyzing public communications needs regarding the proposed action, informing the public, and soliciting feedback. Furthermore, NEPA and its implementing regulations prescribe processes for citizens to appeal proposed activities at multiple levels within the federal agency.

The impact of NEPA procedural requirements is substantial. In Ohio, a state forest official who previously worked for the USDA Forest Service said that NEPA represents one of the biggest differences between state and federal forest policymaking because the law leads to battles over procedures, whereby interested parties can stop proposed forest management activities. In fact, one official on the Wayne National Forest remarked that unless the letter of the law is followed perfectly in planning any given timber sale, an environmental group will successfully appeal the sale under NEPA. In Indiana, all three timber sales proposed on Hoosier National Forest between 1991 and 1995 were appealed, significantly delaying harvests. Appeals substantially affect forest management activities, as described by one federal official:

> The biggest impact of the appeals process is not the time it takes to prepare a response but rather the delay it causes in our activities and the fact that we spend a lot of time and money—hundreds of thousands of dollars—on the front end, trying to design appeal-proof projects. The actual benefits to all of this front end work are minimal. It's a paper exercise that doesn't affect quality of work on the ground. We don't get a lot of return for our investment in the paperwork.

Similarly, federal officials in the Pacific Northwest cited NEPA as one of the most important laws affecting their work. One official on Gifford Pinchot National Forest explained that NEPA requirements affect every project and that they are the primary reason for the forest's thirty-member planning team. Another explained that more than twenty-five appeals were filed in fiscal year 1995: "We were upheld in every case, but nevertheless the appeals impact our work. We have to collect information to send to the regional office to defend each appeal." Appeals also are influential for nontimber activities, as one federal official described:

> I gained millions of dollars in grant funding for a motorized trail reconstruction project to widen trails to increase motorized use, but an anti-motorized use group appealed and we lost on minor points in the process. We'll lose most of the grant money and have to start over—it's frustrating because the lawyers were running the show.

Forest officials in three of the four states, by contrast, are not bound by law to inform the public about proposed forest management actions. There is no "state NEPA" law in Ohio, Indiana, or Oregon, so neither environmental impact statements nor environmental assessments must be made available to the public. Moreover, in these states there is no procedure in place for granting concerned individuals the opportunity to appeal administratively forest officials' decisions. This difference in planning requirements provides state officials with fewer prescribed procedures. As one state official who once worked for the USDA Forest Service noted,

One of the biggest differences between the state Department of Forestry and the Forest Service is the lower amount of planning work here. Each project and decision on a national forest requires NEPA documentation. Here there is no state NEPA, so much less documentation is required and we can move a project through to completion quicker.

In Washington, state officials do face a "state NEPA" statute, but it is less constraining than the NEPA requirements that federal officials face. A key difference is the threshold for determination of when an environmental assessment must be completed. On Washington state forests, only timber sales of more than $100,000 in value require preparation of an assessment. This provision contrasts with USDA Forest Service application of NEPA on the Gifford Pinchot National Forest, which requires an environmental assessment for any timber sale. Moreover, the state law is not regarded as an effective tool for people who oppose projects to cause officials to halt or modify them. Grounds for appeal are limited to certain resource impacts, and the process isn't well-known by the public; thus, appeals filed under the law are rare: None were filed in fiscal year 1995 despite the sale of more than 600 million board-feet of timber. A Washington state citizen with environmental concerns concurred: "The state NEPA law is more watered down than the federal NEPA."

Overall, state officials face fewer requirements than do federal officials to involve the public in forest planning. Thus, state officials have more discretion in determining forest management activities. This is not to say, however, that state officials are isolated from public opinion. Instead, the influence is likely to come through channels other than the planning process. For example, it may be felt through interested publics contacting their state legislators to restrict certain forest agency activities. With regard to legal constraints, however, the important distinction is that, unlike federal officials, state officials generally are not required to inform the public in planning processes.

Limits on Forest Activities on the Ground

As discussed above, laws pertaining to planning processes constrain federal officials more than state officials. Examination of requirements relating to forest activities on the ground yields similar results; federal officials face more legal constraints. Moreover, federal laws foster greater efforts for environmental protection at the federal level, whereas state laws foster greater efforts for timber provision at the state level. Substantive requirements compared in this analysis include statutes mandating the purposes for which forests shall be managed, as well as other statutes and regulations that describe what management tools and techniques must, may, or must not be used in the forests.

Mandates   The Multiple-Use, Sustained-Yield Act (MUSYA) of 1960 directs the U.S. Forest Service to manage national forests for multiple uses—including outdoor recreation, range, timber, watershed, and wildlife and fish—and declares that wilderness areas are consistent with these uses. It directs management to produce the combination of uses that will best meet the needs of the American people "without impairment of the productivity of the land," which is "not necessarily the combination of uses that will give the greatest dollar return or the greatest unit output" (16 USCA Sec. 528–31). In fact, maximization of economic returns was rejected by a federal court ruling that upheld the legality of Forest Service officials selling timber at a net economic loss (*Thomas v. Peterson*, 753 F.2d 754 [9th Cir. 1985]).

In three of the four states I studied, the state forest agency also is required, by state law, to manage its forests for multiple uses (see Table 6.1). Unlike the federal mandate, however, these multiple use mandates do not indicate that timber uses are to be weighted equally with other uses. Instead, these mandates give timber and the revenue it generates greater emphasis than does the federal mandate.

In Ohio, statutory language addressing Ohio state forests lists the following purposes for which the state agency must manage forests: watershed and soil protection, timber production and use, recreation, esthetics, and wildlife habitat (1994 Ohio Code 1503.011). The same state statute, however, directs the agency to take measures to promote

Table 6.1. Elements of Agency's Statutory Mandate Related to
Management Purposes

Explicitly Stated Elements	USFS	Ohio State	Indiana State	Washington State	Oregon State
Multiple uses	x	x	x	x	
Timber	x	x	x	x	
Watershed/soil	x	x	x	x	
Wildlife/fish	x	x	x	x	
Wilderness	x				
Range	x				
Recreation	x	x		x	
Scenic		x		x	
Profitable timber		x			
Produce revenue			x	x	x

"profitable growth of timber" (1994 Ohio Code 1503.03–5). Thus, although the state statute shares a multiple-use mandate with the federal statute, unlike the federal directive it also mandates timber production to generate a profit.

In Indiana, statutory language addressing Indiana state forests
mandates that the state agency protect and conserve timber, water resources, wildlife, and soil for use by current and future generations. It
also mandates, however, that the agency produce timber to improve
the commercial value of the forest, provide revenue to the state and
local governments, and supply local timber markets (Indiana Code 14-
5-4-1, Sec.1; PL1-1995 16-23-4-1). Clearly this emphasis on timber
production to provide revenue differs from that in the federal
mandate.

In Washington, statutory language addressing Washington state
forests includes a multiple-use mandate for the state agency, but this
mandate is tempered by the primary obligation to manage state forest lands for designated trust beneficiaries. The trust mandate, which
is not present in Ohio or Indiana, is common in western states that
have gained statehood within the past 150 years.[3] The state multiple-
use law in Washington lists numerous uses for which the forest agency
shall manage state forests, as long as such uses do not interfere with

the financial obligations of trust management to produce revenue. In addition to timber, multiple uses include recreation, education, scientific studies, special events, hunting and fishing, scenic values, historical sites, watershed protection, and greenbelt areas (Washington Code 79.68.050). As one state official explained, however, "Our mandate is quite different than that of the Forest Service. Public use and nontimber resources are secondary to timber production, due to our fiduciary obligation to generate revenue for the trusts."

In Oregon, no multiple use mandate exists for Oregon state forests. Instead, the mandate is to manage for the predominant use of timber production, to generate revenue for the trusts (Oregon Revised Statute 530.500).[4]

Specific Management Activities   Beyond statutory mandates relating to management purposes, legislation also may constrain specific agency activities. In all four forest pairs, federal forest officials face greater legal substantive restrictions than do state officials, primarily through the NFMA. In addition to the aforementioned planning constraints, the NFMA and its implementing regulations place many constraints on national forest management activities on the ground, including silvicultural techniques, calculation of maximum harvest levels, and species protection.

The NFMA constrains the choice of silvicultural techniques on national forests. Specifically, even-aged silvicultural techniques[5] are allowed only where they are appropriate to meet Plan objectives; reviewed by an interdisciplinary team that considers the potential environmental, economic, esthetic, engineering, and economic impacts; performed in such a manner as to blend with the natural terrain; set within maximum acreage limits; and carried out to be consistent with other multiple uses (16 USCA 1604g3f).

Furthermore, the NFMA stipulates that harvest levels normally must be limited to "sustained yield" amounts, averaged over a ten-year period (16 USCA 1611a). USDA Forest Service regulations have interpreted "sustained yield" to mean nondeclining even flow—a conservative level that assures that no more timber will be harvested in a single year than in the next year, even if variation in harvest levels would generate greater economic returns.[6]

In addition to timber concerns, the NFMA requires federal officials to protect species diversity:

[The Plan must] provide for diversity of plant and animal communities based on the suitability and capability of the specific land area in order to meet overall multiple-use objectives, and . . . provide, where appropriate, to the degree practicable, for steps to be taken to preserve the diversity of tree species similar to that existing in the region controlled by the plan (16 USCA 1604g3b).

This constraint is more than a planning process requirement. Not only does it require officials to discuss species diversity in the Plan, it also requires officials to preserve species diversity. Agency regulations interpreting this requirement have increased its stringency further, requiring that fish and wildlife habitat must be managed to maintain viable populations of native and nonnative species of vertebrates (Hoberg 1997). Thus, officials are not permitted to sell timber in a way that reduces species diversity or threatens the maintenance of viable populations of certain species.

Unlike federal officials, state officials in Ohio and Indiana face few legal requirements regarding silvicultural techniques, harvest levels, or species protection. As one Ohio state official explained, "We have created most of our silviculture parameters, not the legislature. We question each other, so there isn't a need for the legislature to question us so much." Another official indicated that most vegetation management constraints are agency policy, not legislative requirements.

An important legal requirement that affects federal officials but not state officials in Ohio is harvest amounts. Ohio state forest officials are not required to limit quantities to sustained-yield, even-flow amounts. Instead, they may harvest greater quantities in one year than another to increase economic returns.

In Ohio, there is a state law relating to non–point-source pollution[7] that pertains to forest practices such as timber harvesting and trail construction, but this law only establishes a voluntary reporting system. The state forest agency has agreed to submit an operations and management plan to the appropriate county soil and water conservation district before each timber sale or trail construction.

In Indiana, state forest officials do not face state laws prescribing or prohibiting specific activities. As one state official commented, "Other than for wetlands activities or earth moving work, there are no significant statutory constraints affecting management activities on state forests." An important difference between state and federal constraints in Indiana relates to harvest quantities. Unlike federal officials, state officials are not required by law to limit harvest quantities to sustained-yield, even-flow amounts.

In the Pacific Northwest forests, state officials face more legal constraints than do their counterparts in the Midwest, but they still face fewer legal constraints than do federal officials. In Washington, a Forest Practices Act (FPA) constrains Washington state forest officials. FPA statutory requirements and implementing regulations apply to state and private forest lands. FPA provisions address activities related to wetlands, roads, riparian areas, chemical applications, and timber operations. For example, officials must complete a mitigation plan before filling more than one-half acre of wetland, and roads must be of specified length and slope. Of particular importance to forest management is the section describing timber harvest methods. This section limits even-aged harvest methods to 240 acres or less and describes the volume and number of trees per acre to retain, the size and number of trees per acre to leave for wildlife enhancement, and reforestation methods (Washington Administrative Code 222–30).

As in the Midwest forests, an important difference between state and federal constraints in Washington lies in timber harvest quantities. Unlike the federal statute, Washington state law does not require officials to limit harvest amounts to sustained-yield, even-flow amounts. Instead, state officials may harvest quantities that are greater in one time period than another, to increase economic returns.

State forest officials in Oregon also work under a forest practices act. Statutory and regulatory restrictions address several activities on state and private forests, including timber operations, chemical applications, sensitive species monitoring, and protection of ecologically significant sites. For example, with regard to timber operations, even-aged harvest methods normally are limited to 120 acres or less, openings of greater than 25 acres require leaving at least four trees per acre, and officials must leave, temporarily, at least fifty trees per acre in designated "sensitive corridors" (Oregon Code 44.527.740, 44.527.675, 44.527.755). As in Washington, however, state legal requirements in Oregon do not require harvest amounts to be limited to sustained-yield, even-flow amounts, which can limit economic returns.

Across the four forest pairs, then, legal requirements place greater constraints on federal officials than state agency officials, limiting their ability to manage forests profitably for higher levels of timber and requiring greater environmental protection in terms of species protection. This finding supports the argument that, in a federal system, policymakers in lower levels of governance emphasize economic development more than do policymakers in higher levels of governance. The pressure for bureaucrats to pursue certain activities does not come directly from the electorate because civil servants are not elected. Instead, elected legislators and executives craft laws to constrain agency decision makers.

Summary of Legal Constraints

In summary, federal officials face a greater number of legal constraints than do state officials. Moreover, laws foster greater attention to environmental protection at the federal level and to timber at the state level. Such differences are evident in planning requirements as well as in constraints on forest management activities on the ground. Table 6.2 summarizes the key statutes affecting forest officials.

On national forests, the NFMA and NEPA establish formal opportunities for citizen involvement, through public notification and comment provisions as well as avenues for citizen appeals, and the NFMA prescribes what the plans must address. State agencies, on the other hand, face fewer requirements constraining officials' planning processes and plan contents. On the ground, federal agency officials face more stringent legal requirements than do state officials, through NFMA requirements that specify harvest methods, timber sale quantity, and species protection activities.

Across all four forest pairs, differences are evident in federal and state agency statutory mandates. Whereas the federal agency's multiple-use statutory mandate requires that forests shall not be man-

Table 6.2. Key Statutes and Implementing Regulations Affecting Officials

Item	USFS	Ohio State	Indiana State	Washington State	Oregon State
Planning process	NFMA,[a] NEPA[b]	—[c]	—	SEPA[d]	—
Plan contents	NFMA	—	—	—	—
Harvest methods	NFMA	—	—	FPA[e]	FPA
Harvest quantity	NFMA	—	—	—	—
Species protection	NFMA	—	—	—	FPA

[a]NFMA = National Forest Management Act.
[b]NEPA = National Environmental Policy Act.
[c]No key statute or regulations indicated by officials.
[d]SEPA = State version of NEPA.
[e]FPA = Forest Practices Act.

aged for the uses that generate the highest dollar return, the state agency's statutory mandate in Ohio includes a directive to manage state forests for the "profitable growth of timber," and the state agency's mandate in Indiana directs the agency to produce timber to generate revenue for the state and local governments. In Washington and Oregon, mandates require the state agency to manage forests in a manner that will generate revenue for trust beneficiaries.

Thus, there is evidence of systematic differences between higher and lower levels of governance. Elected officials attempt to influence bureaucratic behavior largely through statutory constraints, fostering or limiting agency officials' pursuit of activities such as timber with substantial, direct economic benefits. In the public forest policy sector, laws encourage economic development more at lower than higher levels of governance. In other policy sectors, where economic development is an important goal, lower levels of governance may be the more appropriate locus of responsibility.

Statutory constraints also have an important indirect effect on policy processes. As I discuss in the following section, these constraints affect planning document contents by defining the scope of participants authorized to participate in creating—and challenging—them.

Forest Plans

In addition to laws, a second type of rule is agency-created planning documents. Agency officials can influence the behavior of their subordinates by creating standard operating procedures and plans that guide their activities (Kaufman 1960). Planning documents reflect the preferences of the individuals who create them. Planning documents created and enforced solely by agency officials may be very different than planning documents created and enforced by agency officials in conjunction with external parties. In fact, strategic legislators with different preferences from those of agency bureaucrats may enact legal requirements to involve external parties in creating and enforcing agency planning documents.

Peterson (1995) argues that planning is less open at lower levels of government, where economic interests dominate. Hence, planning documents at higher levels of governance should reflect more input from parties outside the agency and thus more constraints on bureaucratic behavior than those at lower levels of governance. Furthermore, planning document constraints at higher levels of governance are expected to include more restrictions on activities that generate substantial, direct economic benefits.

Substantively, the NFMA-required "land and resource management plans" for national forests are subject, by law, to formal public participation requirements, involving a wide range of interests. These plans are legally enforceable, and environmental groups have brought lawsuits against nearly every national forest plan created under the NFMA. At the state level, in contrast, the degree to which forest agency officials face statutory requirements about planning, and what substantive requirements these mandates contain, are unknown.

In general, planning documents contain rules for certain practices, including timber stand improvement (TSI), "leave trees," riparian area protection, and regeneration harvesting, and they prescribe land management zones. My analysis reveals that federal forest officials face greater constraints than do state officials from planning documents. This difference is especially evident in requirements that promote nontimber goals.

Timber Stand Improvement

TSI activities, which ordinarily involve fertilization and removal of vegetation to increase growth in preferred trees, are subject to guidelines in the agencies' planning documents. In two of the four forest pairs, the federal agency faces more requirements to seek nontimber benefits in TSI activities.

In Ohio, there is a significant difference between state and federal TSI guidelines. For state forests, officials must prioritize TSI activities on the basis of the relative rate of return on the investment. In contrast, federal officials must prioritize TSI activities on the basis not only of financial considerations but also "snag" management needs and other resource considerations. (A snag is a standing, dead tree that may provide useful ecosystem benefits such as wildlife habitat.)

In Indiana, there are no significant differences between state and federal planning TSI requirements. The state document describes the goal of TSI activities as "to produce quality timber and maintain forest health, consistent with other forest benefits including wildlife, recreation, and watershed protection." The national forest Plan is similarly general, providing little specific guidance for TSI activities. For land in the timber base (the area of forest in which commercial timber sales are permitted), the Plan allows TSI work involving tree removal to enhance growth in young hardwood stands, vine control, and stand thinning.

In Washington, state-federal differences are evident. The state planning document requires officials to perform TSI activities on "stands which will respond and produce an acceptable rate of return on investment," with the further stipulation that "the benefits must exceed the costs of fertilizing, thinning, and pruning." The federal Plan, on the other hand, addresses criteria beyond economic costs and returns. It requires officials to prioritize TSI activities "based upon stand condition, requirements for silvicultural prescription, and levels of benefits [not just economic] expected."

In Oregon, the broad state planning document that guides management of Oregon state forests is less specific than the state planning documents in any of the other forest pairs. The document does not address TSI activities, though lower-level forest plans may specify them. Meanwhile, the federal Plan includes economic and noneconomic criteria in its TSI requirements. Thus, no substantial state-federal differences are evident in this pair.

Leave Trees

A significant difference in constraints for environmental protection relates to "leave trees"—trees left standing in a timber harvest area. Such leave trees can provide valuable ecosystem benefits, particularly in terms of habitat. Management to maximize timber provision typically does not involve leaving trees because removal can provide additional timber as well as space for new tree growth. Thus, "leave tree" requirements represent a reduction in timber provision to provide ecosystem benefits. Across the four forest pairs, federal planning documents constrain officials' freedom to remove all trees within a given area more than do state planning documents.

In Ohio, the state forests planning document does not specify the quantity of trees to be left in a harvest area. Instead, individual foresters on the ground exercise their own judgment in determining how many and which trees to leave in a harvest area. In contrast, the Wayne National Forest Plan specifies the average number of trees to be left in each management zone. Similarly, in Indiana the state forests planning document does not address leave tree quantities, whereas the Hoosier National Forest Plan requires that trees for wildlife purposes be left in all stands in the timber base.

In the Pacific Northwest, federal and state planning documents include "leave tree" requirements. The federal Plan provides somewhat stricter requirements. Washington state forest officials must leave, on each acre, a minimum of three trees that are at least ten feet tall and one foot in diameter, depending on the needs of cavity nesting birds, plus two smaller "recruitment" trees and two downed logs per acre in the western portion of the state. Meanwhile, the Gifford Pinchot National Forest Plan requires officials to retain, per acre, at least 15 percent of the trees associated with a stand, in sufficient quantity to support eight listed cavity-nesting bird species at 40 percent of their potential population levels and two listed cavity-nesting bird species at 100 percent of their potential population levels. Standing, dead trees to be left on the national forest must be at least seventeen inches in diameter and forty feet tall. At least 240 linear feet of logs at least 20 feet long and 20 inches in diameter at the large end must be left.

Because a single Douglas fir tree may grow to 240 feet in height, it is not clear whether requiring 240 linear feet of logs, as the federal Plan does, is greater or less than requiring two downed logs, as the state planning document does. For standing leave trees, however, the federal Plan's requirement to retain at least 15 percent of a stand is greater than the state planning document's requirement to retain at least five standing trees per acre. Moreover, the federal Plan requires that standing, dead trees be at least forty feet tall, compared to the state planning document minimum requirement of only ten feet for standing, reserve trees.

In Oregon, state forest officials must leave, on average per acre, a minimum of two standing trees at least thirty feet tall and eleven inches in diameter at breast height, plus two downed logs each at least ten cubic feet and six feet long. Meanwhile, the federal Plan requires federal officials to retain leave trees at least twenty feet tall and twenty inches in diameter at breast height, in sufficient quantity to support at least 40 percent of the potential population level of specified cavity-nesting birds. Federal officials also must leave, per acre, a minimum of two downed logs each at least forty cubic feet in volume and twelve feet in length. Although requirements for standing trees to be left are not comparable across the agencies (state requirements are described in terms of number of trees, whereas federal requirements are described in terms of habitat sufficiency), requirements for downed logs can be compared. The federal Plan requirement to leave down trees that are forty cubic feet in volume and twelve feet in length is four times the volume and twice the average length per acre as the state planning document requirement.

Riparian Areas

Riparian areas are lands that serve as a transition between aquatic and terrestrial ecosystems. Forest management activities may negatively affect riparian areas as soil is compacted, vegetation is removed, and roads or trails are established. In a majority of the forest pairs, federal officials face more stringent plan requirements than do state officials to protect riparian areas.

In Ohio, the federal Plan places restrictions on activities in riparian areas that are similar to those in the state planning document. Federal requirements for activities near any intermittent or perennial streams include minimum "filter strip" (buffer) widths on which earth-disturbing activities are not allowed unless special techniques are used. These minimum widths are based on an area's slope and site sensitivity. Moreover, operators may leave logging debris in permanent waters only where they benefit fisheries habitat or protect riparian values. The state planning manual requires minimum filter strip widths that are based on an area's slope, which are similar to federal minimum width requirements.

In Indiana, the federal Plan forbids commercial timber harvesting in riparian areas, except "to enhance or maintain riparian-dependent resources, to permit development of recreation access facilities, to provide for utilities, or to protect public safety." The state planning document, on the other hand, allows multiple-use management in riparian areas, including commercial timber production, although nontimber resources are to be emphasized. Moreover, the federal Plan specifies a more inclusive definition of riparian areas, including all watercourses regardless of flow (i.e., intermittent streams are included), whereas the state planning document includes only permanently flowing waters.

Similarly, in Washington, federal officials face stricter riparian protection requirements than do state officials. The federal Plan prohibits commercial timber harvest in riparian areas, whereas the state planning document allows timber harvest in riparian areas. In addition, the federal Plan requires protection of all permanent as well as intermittent streams, whereas the state planning document requires protection primarily for permanent streams.

In Oregon, riparian protection requirements also are more stringent in the federal Plan than in the state planning document. The federal Plan establishes buffer zones, called "riparian reserves," of approximately 520 feet on either side of perennial streams and 260 feet on either side of intermittent streams. Commercial timber harvests are prohibited within the buffers.

Riparian protection requirements in the Oregon state forest planning document come from Forest Practices Act implementing regulations, which specify a range of buffer widths. In 1994, the agency developed a set of comprehensive riparian regulations aiming to allow timber harvest while protecting fish and wildlife habitat and water quality. Riparian widths on each side of a stream depend on stream size (small, medium, or large) and use (game fish, other fish, or domestic water use by a water permit holder). The most protective category is large streams with game fish or with other fish plus domestic water use. In this category, the buffer is 100 feet. The least protective category is small streams without game fish or domestic water use, which require no buffer. Within buffer areas, commercial timber harvesting is allowed, as long as a specified number of trees are left standing. Thus, compared to federal Plan requirements, state riparian protection is less restrictive in terms of buffer size and activities permitted within buffers.

Regeneration Harvesting

Silvicultural techniques describe methods used in harvesting timber. One somewhat controversial method is "regeneration harvesting,"— also called "clearcutting"—which involves removal of all trees within an area to create a forest opening for trees to grow.[8] Most foresters consider regeneration harvesting to be beneficial for promoting the growth of shade-intolerant species (those requiring substantial sunlight), many of which provide high-value timber, and for providing habitat that is favorable to certain wildlife species. Many foresters recognize the esthetic drawbacks of regeneration harvesting, however, and numerous environmentalists have protested that this method damages forest ecosystems. Broadly speaking, regeneration harvesting promotes economic development of the timber resource while potentially detracting from esthetic values and forest ecosystem conditions. In my analysis, I find that federal planning documents tend to restrict regeneration harvesting more than do state planning documents. Federal documents mandate smaller areas where regeneration harvesting is allowed and smaller maximum opening sizes allowed in carrying out regeneration harvesting

In Ohio, the federal Plan allows openings up to thirty acres on 35 percent of the forest, whereas the state plan allows openings up to twenty-five acres, or forty acres with central office approval, on 62 percent of the forest. In Indiana, however, state restrictions are somewhat stricter than federal restrictions; state officials may create openings of up to five acres, or larger with central office approval, on 55 percent of the forest, whereas the federal Plan allows openings of up to ten acres on 55 percent of the forest. In Washington, aside from aforementioned riparian restrictions, about 51 percent of national forest land is available for openings, compared to 90 percent of state forest land. Moreover, the federal Plan restricts openings to 60 or 40 acres, depending on dominant species type, whereas the state planning document restricts openings to 100 acres. In Oregon, aside from riparian restrictions, opening creation is permitted on 18 percent of national forest but 98 percent of state forest land. Opening size is limited to 60 or 40 acres on the national forest, depending on dominant species type, but 120 acres on state forests.

Land-Use Zones

Like regeneration harvesting restrictions, land-use zoning restrictions are a helpful indicator for comparing agency planning document emphasis on economic development as opposed to noneconomic benefits. Federal and state forest planning documents across the forest pairs include designated zones in which timber harvesting and other commodity production activities are not a primary activity. In three of the four pairs, a higher proportion of land area is zoned as protected area in the national forest than in the state forest.

In Ohio, about 11 percent of national forest land is in protected areas, where programmed timber harvesting is not allowed and management focuses on resource protection or dispersed recreation. A similar proportion of state forest land—about 13 percent—is so zoned. In the other pairs, however, differences are evident. In Indiana, about 33 percent of the national forest has been zoned in the forest plan as protected area, compared to just 4 percent of state forest land. In

Washington, the federal Plan designates a substantial portion (42 percent) of the forest as "late successional reserve," where management must focus on the creation of late successional forest conditions—with trees more than eighty years old, a multiple-layered canopy, and substantial volumes of down and dead material remaining on the forest floor. In contrast, only about 10 percent of state forest land has been designated off-limits to standard timber provision. In Oregon, 81 percent of national forest acreage is designated "late successional reserve," whereas only about 2 percent of the state forest acreage is off-limits to standard harvesting.

Explaining Differences in Planning Document Constraints

In general, planning documents in each forest pair specify more constraints overall—and more constraints that foster noneconomic activities such as environmental protection—at the federal level than at the state level. As Table 6.3 summarizes, for the first indicator (timber stand improvement) the federal agency planning document includes stricter requirements for environmental protection in two forest pairs; requirements are similar in the other two pairs. For the second indicator ("leave trees"), however, the federal planning document is stricter in all pairs. For the third indicator (riparian areas), the federal planning document is stricter in three pairs, and requirements are similar in one pair. For the fourth indicator (regeneration openings), the federal planning document is stricter in three pairs, and the state planning document is stricter in one pair. For the fifth indicator (land-use zone restrictions), the federal planning document is stricter in three pairs, and requirements are similar in one pair.

Planning documents are created with consideration of conditions on the ground in particular forests. Thus, documents reflect the physical characteristics of a given forest. Nevertheless, the systematic differences between state and federal planning documents cannot convincingly be explained by physical differences between forests. As I indicate in chapter 2, selection of forests within each pair emphasized forests with similar physical attributes. Thus, we must turn to other reasons to understand such marked differences in planning document constraints.

Table 6.3. Summary of Restrictions Included in Planning Documents

Activity or Condition	Agency Facing More Requirements for Environmental Protection			
	Ohio	Indiana	Washington	Oregon
Timber stand improvement	Federal	Similar	Federal	Similar
Leave trees	Federal	Federal	Federal	Federal
Riparian areas	Similar	Federal	Federal	Federal
Regeneration openings	Federal	State	Federal	Federal
Zone restrictions	Similar	Federal	Federal	Federal

An important explanation for the systematic differences in planning document constraints involves public input. Development of the national forest Plans involved a wide variety of interests, including environmentalists, trail riders, hikers, timber harvesters, oil and gas producers, bird watchers, and others. As specified in the NFMA, all of these groups had access to the national forest Plans during formulation; thus, they pursued their preferences with officials who were creating the planning documents.

Outside interests had less influence in state forest planning documents. In fact, in Ohio and Indiana, such documents were formulated exclusively by agency officials, without significant citizen input. Although these officials may have tried earnestly to take multiple uses into account, they did not face the same statutorily mandated involvement from people favoring environmental protection as did federal officials. Even in Washington and Oregon, which held several public meetings in the state forest planning processes, citizens had less power to pursue their preferences through legally sanctioned channels in state planning than in federal planning.

The lower level of environmental protection requirements at the state level has not gone unnoticed by environmental communities. For example, in 1995 a group of environmentalists in Ohio began to press for greater inclusion in state planning processes, perceiving that a more open approach to planning might lead to planning document constraints that provide greater environmental protection than did existing ones.

Greater citizen input in federal agency planning is evident in more than just planning document creation. Citizens also have greater input in federal agency plan enforcement and amendment. Although officials' compliance with planning restrictions is monitored by their supervisors in federal as well as state agencies, only in national forests are the restrictions subject to challenges by outside parties, with the power to force judicial review. Planning document requirements are legally binding on federal officials, and changes to a national forest Plan are not valid unless they are made through a formal amendment process. State planning documents, on the other hand, are not legally enforceable by outside parties, and the documents may be amended internally, without citizen input.

These differences in planning document formulation and amendment lead to the federal-state differences described in this chapter. Namely, federal planning documents specify more constraints on officials than do state planning documents, and these constraints emphasize greater environmental protection on national forests than on state forests.

Conclusion

Bureaucratic behavior theory suggests several factors to explain agency officials' policymaking. One such factor—rules—provides a means for elected officials and higher-level agency personnel to influence agency officials. As predicted by the functional theory of federalism, elected officials have constrained forest agency officials to a greater degree at the federal level than at the state level, and such constraints have restricted federal officials more than state officials' ability to pursue economic development through timber provision.

The most significant legal constraints in public forest policy are the NFMA and NEPA, both of which require agency officials to undertake specified planning processes that give power to citizens. National forest timber sales are routinely held up as citizen suits seek injunctions on the basis of procedural questions in the planning process. This finding supports Hoberg's (1992) argument that federal agency environmental policymaking in the past three decades has been marked by legal constraints that reduce bureaucratic autonomy and provide citizens pursuing nonbusiness interests greater opportunities to engage in policymaking. Hoberg (1997) contrasts USDA Forest Service policymaking before and after the 1970s: The earlier period was dominated by bureaucrats who faced few legal constraints on timber provision and tended to favor local timber interests. Results from the study at hand suggest that state forest policy in the 1990s paralleled national forest policy in the 1970s, in the sense that state forest agencies did not face environmental interests with potent legal hammers.

State-federal differences also are apparent in on-the-ground limits. The federal statutory mandates emphasize multiple forest uses and management that is not based on economic returns, whereas state mandates emphasize timber production and economic returns. The NFMA stipulates certain requirements for silvicultural techniques, maximum harvest levels, and species protection, all of which promote environmental protection over economic production, whereas the states face minimal substantive legal requirements that would diminish timber provision and revenue generation.

The second type of rule—forest plans—exhibits a similar state-federal difference. As evidenced by plan requirements for TSI, "leave trees," riparian area protection, regeneration harvesting, and protective zoning, federal forest officials face greater constraints, especially on timber provision, from their planning documents than do state officials. Because forest plans are not created by elected officials, the functional theory of federalism does not explain this difference directly.

Elected officials have affected plan contents indirectly, however, by determining who is authorized to participate in creating forest plans. At the federal level, citizens can block proposed agency plans through administrative and judicial appeals. In fact, nearly every national forest plan has been appealed, typically by citizens opposing timber harvests. Such citizen power encourages agency officials developing forest plans to provide increased environmental protection, even at the expense of economic development.

Elected officials also can influence agency officials' policymaking through another type of rule: budget incentives. I examine this possibility in chapter 7.

Notes

1. It is important to note the distinction between planning process requirements, which constrain how officials go about creating their planning documents, and the resulting constraints in the completed planning documents themselves (I discuss the latter extensively subsequently in this chapter). For example, a planning process requirement may demand that agency officials specify zones on the forest in which timber harvesting will occur. A completed planning document that is in compliance with such a process requirement would include maps showing where timber zones have been designated on the forest.

2. The committee is composed of eight members, representing forest-based research activities, small private forest owners, large private forest owners, the pulp and paper industry, other forest industries, soil science, forest recreation, and the public.

3. For a thorough description of state trust lands, see Souder and Fairfax (1996).

4. Oregon Revised Statute 530.500 lists a variety of uses for state forest lands, but it does not provide a multiple-use mandate. Instead, the statute declares, "The State Forester may permit use of lands for other [nontimber] purposes," including fish and wildlife, landscape, protection against flood and erosion, recreation, and water supply protection. Of course, permission ("may") to manage for multiple uses does not constitute a mandate ("must" or "shall").

5. Even-aged management is defined statutorily as "the application of a combination of actions that results in the creation of stands in which trees of essentially the same age grow together." Clearcutting is one tool for even-aged management.

6. There are two primary reasons that even-flow requirements limit economic returns. First, harvesting a higher level of timber in the present can open space in the forest that is necessary for growing new trees that require sunlight, which may have a faster growth rate than older trees. Second, harvesting a higher level of timber at a period when market prices are high can increase economic returns.

7. Non–point-source pollution is pollution emanating from dispersed activities rather than a single source such as a pipe or smokestack.

8. Large openings often are called "clearcuts," whereas smaller clearings may be termed "gaps" or "group selection openings," but there is no universally agreed size definition to distinguish the two.

7 Budget Incentives

Chapter 6 describes four themes from theories explaining bureaucratic behavior. The first of these themes—rules—includes laws and forest plans, which elected officials are able to influence. In keeping with the functional theory of federalism, compared to the state level, elected officials at the federal level have created laws affecting planning processes and on-the-ground activities that make it harder for federal forest agency officials to pursue economic development. The forest plans themselves reflect these differences, as greater citizen authority at the federal level has led to national forest plan requirements that make timber provision more difficult than it is on state forests.

In this chapter I discuss the third type of rule: budget incentives. Like laws and forest plans, budgets provide an avenue for elected officials to influence agency policymaking, by determining agency appropriations as well as by creating budget incentives relating to timber and nontimber revenues generated on public forests. It turns out that state and federal agency budget incentives are not systematically different from each other.

The Role of Budget Incentives in Bureaucratic Behavior

The importance of budget incentives in explaining agency policymaking is a mainstay of bureaucratic behavior theory. Starting with the assumption that bureaucrats with budgetary discretion seek to maximize their revenues, rather than simply to follow the goals set by agency superiors or legislators, models have depicted the circumstances under which the agent (i.e., the person to whom authority is delegated) could be controlled by the principal (the delegator), in the face of the agent's information advantage (Niskanen 1971; Ross 1973; for a review, see Bendor 1990). These models assume that bureaucrats' behavior is shaped largely by their budget incentives, which depend on institutional arrangements that affect how officials acquire revenue needed to perform forest management activities. These arrangements provide incentives for budget-motivated officials who are interested in budget maximization or maintenance to behave in certain ways to acquire desired levels of revenue.

The notion of perverse budget incentives that encourage forest officials to overharvest timber is widespread in descriptions of the USDA Forest Service. Analysts typically cite the Knutsen-Vandenberg Act (K-V Act) of 1930, which provides for each national forest to share revenue from timber sales on that forest (see, for example, Budiansky 1991; O'Toole 1988; Rice 1989). They conclude that this incentive leads to higher timber sales, assuming that its budgetary "carrots" strongly influence forest officials to sell more timber than they otherwise would.

Although timber budget incentives arguably are the most well-documented, they are not the only means by which budgets might influence bureaucratic behavior. Agency officials who desire to increase or maintain their budget resources are expected to seek opportunities to obtain revenue from nontimber uses, as well as from general appropriations. Such opportunities can be compared at the state and federal levels.

It is important to note that, for budget incentives to motivate behavior, individuals must believe that their actions can influence their budget allocations. Thus, I begin by investigating how and whether officials believe they can increase their funding, through appropriations and revenue collected from forest users. My analysis indicates that current federal and state budget processes do not encourage such a belief; officials do not generally see a substantial link between their behavior and their budgets.

Appropriations

At the federal level as well as the state level, agency officials receive appropriations from the annual or biennial budgets passed by the legislature and signed by the chief executive (president or governor). Budgetary resources subsequently are split among forest agency headquarters and regional and field offices. To determine the importance of appropriations incentives in shaping officials' behavior, it is necessary to understand the appropriations process and the degree to which officials perceive that their actions can affect their appropriations. Analysis of these items does not support the functional theory of federalism's expectation—that budget incentives systematically encourage state officials to emphasize activities such as selling timber that generate substantial, direct economic benefits more than federal officials.

Ohio

The operating appropriations process for Ohio state forests begins with the state forest agency submitting a budget request to the state natural resources department, which subsequently submits a budget to the governor's budget office. The forest agency competes with other agencies in the natural resources department for its share of budgetary resources, and it supports requests for the overall department budget allocation once that budget has been prepared. The governor's budget office formulates the governor's budget to be presented to the state legislature, which makes alterations and eventually passes, for the governor's signature, a two-year lump sum allocation that includes funding for forest agency operations.

Some state forest officials in Ohio indicated that they might improve their chances of appropriations success through a variety of strategies. One forest official who is closely involved with the budget process indicated that factors that are important for success include providing "solid" forestry programs; maintaining good relationships with agency constituents who can lobby legislators for higher funding; developing a strong identity for the forest agency to set it apart from other natural resource agencies; and, to a lesser extent, showing financial profit from forest operations. Another state official with agency budget responsibilities noted the importance of constituent pressure on legislators to increase the natural resources department's appropriations. Although the legislature does not allocate specific line-item amounts within an agency, forest officials let legislators know which items would be cut in cases of funding shortfalls.

Officials at lower levels of the state forest agency compete with other parts of the agency for funds. They cited several potentially useful strategies to increase their revenues, including saving money in one area to transfer to another, showing that the additional revenue will generate more revenue or save money, and demonstrating that the additional revenue will improve work quality or accuracy. Among these various strategies cited by higher and lower state officials, only one individual mentioned showing profit from forest operations, and he said that this was not a primary strategy.

Although some state officials in Ohio perceive their activities to be linked to appropriations levels, several others stated that there is little they can do to increase their funding appropriations because allocations are largely incremental. They remarked that, no matter what activities they undertake, their budget sum would be based primarily on past allocation levels. In fact, regional and local officials pointed to budgets that had not increased in several years. Moreover, budget changes are more likely to result from uncontrollable physical variables such as fires, weather, or pest infestations than from officials' behavior.

For the federal forest agency in Ohio, the appropriations process for the operating budget begins with program managers developing project work plans and estimating budget needs for about forty "expanded budget line items." Members of the forest "leadership team," which comprises a dozen individuals—including program managers, district rangers, budgeting support staff, and the forest supervisor— meet to compile the forest budget request. This request is submitted to the appropriate USDA Forest Service regional office (in this case, in Milwaukee, Wisconsin) and, subsequently, combined into a regional budget that is sent to the Washington, D.C., headquarters of the Forest Service, to be submitted to the Office of Management and Budget (OMB) for integration into the president's budget request to Congress. Eventually Congress passes an appropriations bill for the pres-

ident's signature, which lists amounts allocated to each of the Forest
Service expanded budget line items.

Once the USDA Forest Service headquarters in Washington receives its appropriations line items, it divides the funds among its nine
regions. At the regional level, a leadership team that includes forest
supervisors in the region divides the regional line-item appropriations
among different forests. One national forest official indicated that
these meetings can include heated debate over amounts allocated to
different forests. Decisions are based primarily on past program levels at each forest and recognized needs. For example, Wayne National
Forest includes a large amount of land that was degraded in the past,
so it receives a large proportion of the region's soil and water restoration funds. Furthermore, forest budget requests come into play; if a
forest requests only a small amount for a certain expanded budget line
item, it is not likely to receive a large appropriation for that item.

On the national forest in Ohio, within-forest priorities must be determined among various programs. One member of the leadership
team said that the sum of the forest's expanded budget line-item requests to the region could not exceed a set figure; thus, individuals had
to compete, in a sense, with other team members on the forest. This
official remarked that useful justifications include linking desired activities to the forest Plan and to user demands and showing how certain expenditures would save money in the long run (e.g., preventa-
tive maintenance of facilities to avoid more costly future repairs).

Although national forest program managers in Ohio may feel some
ability to affect their budget appropriations within the forest's appropriations, they also recognize the larger constraint from the forest's
total appropriation. One official indicated that, in submitting the forest budget to the USDA Forest Service regional office, there was little
he could do to increase the forest-level budget because the primary
factors for determining allocations are past appropriations and congressional and executive priorities. This official also mentioned the importance of emphasizing special conditions on the forest. Obviously,
forest conditions such as past land degradation cannot readily be
changed by officials desiring higher appropriations.

Federal officials' sense of inability to influence appropriations levels in Ohio is compounded by the lengthy budgeting process, which

clashes with constantly changing executive and legislative political priorities. Federal officials typically work on budget requests for three years in the future; in the fall of 1995, management team members were preparing the fiscal year 1998 budget request. This long lead time makes it difficult to predict which line items Congress will prioritize. For example, if Congress were to increase wildlife funding and the management team had not requested a large wildlife allocation, the forest would miss out on extra funds.

Indiana

Officials on Indiana state forests at the forest level prepare a budget request that includes estimated amounts for annual operating expenses on the forest, plus funding requests for a variety of specific projects. The request is passed up to agency officials who compile requests from each forest, prioritize needs, and create an agency budget request that is submitted to the natural resources department. The natural resources department, in turn, submits a budget request to the governor's office for consideration in the governor's request to the state legislature. Eventually the legislature passes a budget, which, when signed by the governor, allocates funds that are suballocated to the department and the forest agency in several broad "budget points": personnel, utilities, services, operating, equipment, workers' compensation, and travel. Funds for specific projects also may be allocated.

State officials in Indiana listed several potential strategies to increase budget success. One field-level forest official said that public contact with legislators or higher state agency officials, in support of specific projects, might lead to higher allocations. He believes that the forest officials who are most successful in securing funding can show that they are using funds efficiently and that they have public support. Another state official indicated that the best chance for increasing his budget would be to have constituent groups ask the legislature for higher funding. Unfortunately, he added, he cannot ensure that such groups do so.

A budgetary strategy that was not mentioned was increasing timber provision. State officials do not perceive a strong link between timber provision and appropriations levels. This finding is surprising in light of the fact that the forest agency has a dedicated fund with forest revenues accruing for future use by the agency. The appropriations process ensures, however, that this dedicated fund does not provide budgetary rewards for increased commodity revenue. After revenues accrue to the dedicated fund, legislative authorizations tend to prevent higher agency earnings from yielding a larger agency budget. One state official explained,

> The dedicated fund comprised about 82 percent of our total operating budget last year [1995]. The legislature has to allocate funds before we can spend them. They nearly always allocate the whole dedicated fund amount, and they add additional general revenue funds needed to provide an overall stable operating budget year to year. There's no budget incentive for us to earn more money from forest activities, since our bottom line won't change—if our revenues go up, the legislature will just reduce the portion of our funding that comes from state general revenues.

Moreover, actions designed to increase forest revenue would require additional labor, which several officials felt their agency could not spare.

Realistically, then, state forest officials see little opportunity to affect their appropriations levels. As one Indiana state forest official said, "We have little influence over our appropriations; by the time our request goes up to the department, the governor, and finally the legislature, there's not much we can do." Another said, "Regardless of our efforts, the operating budget is not likely to change from year to year."

Federal officials in Indiana face a budgeting process that is similar to that described by federal officials in Ohio. Budget team members on the national forest negotiate among each other to produce a "constrained" line-item budget that doesn't exceed a predetermined maximum amount for the forest. This request is sent up to the regional office, where it is consolidated with other forests' requests and passed on to the USDA Forest Service headquarters in Washington, D.C., which consolidates it with the requests from other regions. The Forest Service budget request eventually passes through OMB and into the president's budget request, then to Congress, which allocates funds in expanded budget line items.

Possible strategies for program managers to secure a larger share of the national forest total in Indiana include showing that the funds will be used to reach Plan objectives, addressing user health and safety issues, and meeting output quantity targets previously approved by the regional office. Such output targets include a variety of forest uses, including timber, wildlife habitat, trails, and recreational sites.

In general, however, federal officials in Indiana see little opportunity to influence their budget. One Hoosier National Forest official described the most important factor for increasing his budget as physical conditions that are beyond his control, such as storm or insect damage that creates a need for treatment. Another federal official explained that, within the forest budget ceiling, it is important not to push too hard to take money from other programs because being a team player in managing the national forest is critical. From a total forest standpoint, one federal official said, "There's not much we can do to improve the budget; in fact, we're in a serious reduction mode now." Moreover, budgets are unpredictable, with the three-year budgeting occurring in an unstable political climate in which it isn't known which line items will be favored by Congress in the future. One Hoosier National Forest official put it succinctly: "It's all politics, not based on our arguments."

Therefore, as in Ohio, evidence from Indiana does not indicate state-federal differences in line with the functional theory of federalism. State officials do not face greater appropriations incentives than federal officials to focus on activities that create substantial, direct economic benefits. In fact, neither state nor federal officials face strong appropriations incentives to undertake any specific management activities as a means to gain higher appropriation levels. Instead, many perceive that appropriation amounts are largely beyond their ability to influence.

Washington

Officials on Washington state forests receive funding from the state general fund as well as from revenue earned through the sale of forest commodities. For either source, the budget allocation must be authorized by the state legislature. When asked to describe helpful strategies for increasing or sustaining budget allocations, several officials suggested the importance of quantifying costs and linking the budget to specific outputs—especially those that generate revenue. For example, one official noted the success of showing that funding to examine cellular phone tower leasing on state forests would more than pay its own way in future revenue. Other state officials indicated that officials whose work is directly tied to timber sales have greater influence than those whose work is not. Although such strategies indicate incentives to generate revenue to receive higher budget allocations, the ability of an official to influence his or her budget should not be overstated. As one official said, "In the budget process, the budget goes through so many people that by the time it gets back to me, I have little influence."

Federal officials on Gifford Pinchot National Forest face a budget process that is similar to that for federal officials on other national forests. In fact, suggested strategies for increasing or protecting their budget mirror those cited by federal officials in Ohio and Indiana. For example, one official on Gifford Pinchot National Forest said that it is important to link funding in specific line items to specific outputs, especially those that improve forest user service or safety. It also is important to request higher amounts for line items that Congress funds more in a particular year. In addition, physical conditions that are beyond the control of the agency are critical: Damage caused by weather can provide an effective justification for additional funds to make repairs. Several officials said that proposed timber activities are likely to have greater funding success, but other resources also may have funding success, including fisheries, watershed restoration, and recreation. In addition, cost savings may be important, if funding can be shown to reduce future costs by preventing facility deterioration.

Despite these possible strategies, several federal officials believe that they have little ability to influence budget amounts. As one national forest official explained, "The budget is more a reflection of last year's budget, with little chance to shape appropriations." Another suggested that, for the timber program, the sale target level determined by the Plan dictated the maximum that would be funded for timber activities, so little influence was possible.

Thus, in the state of Washington, federal officials described a mix of strategies for obtaining funds, including emphasizing timber activities but also several other strategies. These descriptions differ from those of state officials in Washington, who suggested primarily that revenue-generating activities were more likely to lead to success in budget levels received. This difference suggests the possibility of state-federal differences, in line with the functional theory of federalism. At both agencies, however, there were individuals who doubted their ability to affect budgets meaningfully.

Oregon

Officials on Oregon state forests seek authorization from the state legislature for their budget. The operational budget is granted in two broad categories—Board of Forestry (county) and School Trust lands—rather than in multiple, narrowly defined line items. Field-level officials request funds from area offices, which request money from the forest agency headquarters in the state capital. In making successful requests, one state official cited the importance of encouraging constituent groups to contact legislators in support of budget requests. (Recall that state officials in Ohio and Indiana also described this strategy.)

Another budget request strategy that Oregon state officials perceive to be successful is focusing on activities that will generate revenue. For example, as one official explained, a successful argument could be made for hiring another forester to increase sale preparation for commercial thinnings, which generate revenue from the trees sold as well as from future increased timber value in thinned stands. Another official stated that the agency usually has "no problem" in receiving requested authorizations, especially if the argument is made that funds will be used to increase intensive management for timber. Certain nontimber activities related to long-range planning—such as developing geographical information systems or inventorying birds, water, and soil—may be similarly likely to receive funding. Other nontimber activities are less likely to receive full funding requests, however. For example, recreation funds were not provided at requested levels during the 1995 budget cycle, reflecting a general desire to reduce government spending.

Federal officials in Oregon expressed less faith in their ability to influence budget request success through any strategy. One Siuslaw National Forest official said, "There's not much we can do to increase our budgets, so we focus on stretching our dollars further." Another said, "I'm pretty cynical about the budget process—which starts from the ground up, but by the time it gets to OMB and Congress and trickles back down in a mystical process, we get amounts decided by people who don't know our situations."

Nevertheless, several national forest officials did cite strategies that may increase appropriations success. For example, proposing additional timber activities may be more successful than other strategies because "Congress likes timber production to create jobs and income for local economies and to supply timber for the nation," in the words of one official. Nevertheless, the agency's timber budget request is constrained by the fact that timber sales are limited to target levels set in the Plan. Other activities with better funding opportunities include those for which planning already has been completed, such as stream restoration and road obliteration.

Thus, in Oregon federal officials expressed somewhat less optimistic views about their ability to influence budgets than did state officials. State officials described a primary strategy as emphasizing how funding would be used to generate revenue, whereas few federal officials described revenue generation as a key to successful budget requests.

Appropriations Summary

Overall, then, the evidence for systematic state-federal differences in budget incentives is not convincing (see Table 7.1). In Washington and Oregon, state officials indicated a stronger link between timber and revenue-generating activities and budget request success than did federal officials. Nevertheless, several state officials in Washington described an inability to influence their budget allocations meaningfully. In Ohio and Indiana, state officials did not describe revenue-generating activities as being significantly linked to budget request success. In fact, neither state nor federal officials in the Midwest forest pairs

Table 7.1. Summary of Officials' Appropriations Incentives

	Agencies with Officials Indicating This Strategy is an Effective Way to Increase Appropriations			
Strategy	*Ohio*	*Indiana*	*Washington*	*Oregon*
Increase timber provision	Neither	Neither	Both	State
Increase other revenue-generating activities	Neither	Neither	State	Neither

indicated substantial efficacy in influencing their budget allocations, regardless of the strategies they pursued. Considering all four pairs, evidence does not indicate substantial differences between state and federal officials for this type of rule. There appear to be some regional differences, however: State officials in the Pacific Northwest cite the strongest appropriations incentives to increase agency revenue and timber provision.

User Payments

Although data regarding budget appropriations do not indicate systematic state-federal differences in budget incentives, it is important to examine all sources of agency revenue. If state and federal officials feel relatively powerless to affect their budget appropriations, perhaps they try to increase revenues from other sources. For example, because many individuals visit the forests to undertake activities such as horse trail riding, off-road vehicle riding, camping, and special forest product collection, use fees might generate additional revenue. Furthermore, commodity production such as timber can generate substantial receipts. On the basis of the functional theory of federalism, one would expect to find greater incentives encouraging revenue generation from user payments on state than national forests. Although this expectation appears, at first, to be supported with regard to non-timber uses, in practice it is not. Nor is this difference apparent for the most significant nonappropriations revenue source—timber sales.

Nontimber Use Fees

Ohio

Ohio state forest officials are allowed to collect and retain certain fees. The state agency chief may set prices and retain revenue for uses such as firewood collection, hiking, camping, and trail riding. Revenues generated from these payments accrue to the forest agency head-quarters in the state capital. Because local and regional state forest officials do not retain such revenues, there is no direct revenue incentive for them to encourage fee-generating activities. Nevertheless, officials at agency headquarters may be motivated by the incentive structure that allows agency retention of such user payments.

This potential motivation is not realized in practice, however; officials do not regard the arrangement as providing an incentive to collect use fees. Despite the rule allowing state forest officials to retain nontimber use fees for agency purposes, these officials recognize that such revenues constitute only a small portion of the agency's revenues. Several officials cited this small contribution, as well as the high cost of collecting the fees, as discouraging efforts to collect more revenue from forest users. No state official suggested that increasing efforts to collect use fees would be a worthwhile endeavor for agency revenue enhancement.

In fact, prior to 1995 the forest agency chief had waived all recreational use fees, for financial reasons of another type: liability. In case of injury, a forest user who has paid a use fee for a trail or campsite on a state forest has a potential liability claim against the forest agency. If no fees are collected, the state is less likely to be liable for costs associated with injuries. Therefore, state forest officials can reduce the potential for large economic losses by waiving use fees. Thus, although the expectation that state forest officials are more likely to encourage use fees is not supported, the underlying theory that state-level officials are highly focused on economic concerns (i.e., financial liability) is supported.

Like state forest officials, federal forest officials in Ohio collect revenue from nontimber forest activities, although rules specifying what fees may be collected are more stringent than those state officials face. Federal law (16 USCA 460 l) specifies that federal forest officials may not collect use fees for entrance into a general area for recreational use (although they may circumvent this rule, to some extent, by charging fees for parking in a recreational area that is not readily accessible without a motorized vehicle). The same law prohibits collection of use fees for camping unless the facilities meet certain minimum standards, including tent or trailer spaces, drinking water, road access, garbage containers, toilets, picnic tables, reasonable visitor protection, and campfire containment devices.

Whereas the state agency in Ohio retains 100 percent of the nontimber use fees it collects, the federal forest agency retains just 15 percent of its nontimber use fees. Furthermore, this revenue is not available for general forest expenditure; it must be reinvested into the resource that generated it—for example, a specific campground. Thus, one federal official indicated that, considering the expense involved in collecting fees and maintaining facilities, increasing use fees would not be an effective way to raise revenue for managing the forest because the net effect would be to lose money. Therefore, like state agency officials, federal officials in Ohio do not face significant incentives to undertake activities to generate revenue from users.

Indiana

Nontimber use fees collected from Indiana state forest users are deposited in a dedicated fund for the state forest agency as a whole. Thus, field-level officials do not gain direct economic benefits from increasing use fee collection. Higher-level agency officials, on the other hand, might be expected to increase use fees if that would translate into higher levels of agency funding. As noted in the appropriations discussion, however, in Indiana the state forestry dedicated fund is not available for agency use until legislators allocate it through the legislative appropriations process. Because legislators tend to appropriate the same total level of funding from year to year, an increase in dedicated fund money would be offset by a decrease in general revenue money. Thus, from agency officials' perspective, there is little budgetary advantage in collecting higher levels of use fees.[1]

Even if state forest agency officials in Indiana did seek to increase use fee revenues, they would be constrained in their ability to do so, for two reasons. First, all use fees on state lands are determined for the entire natural resources department. One forest official explained, "The parks division takes the lead in establishing visitor fees such as camping on all state properties." Second, in 1995 Governor Evan Bayh initiated a reduction in use fees statewide, cutting many by as much as 50 percent and eliminating others entirely. Thus, without budgetary benefits associated with increased use fees, and with limits on their ability to set use fee rates, state officials do not have budget incentives to increase use fee collection.

Nor do federal forest officials in Indiana face incentives to increase nontimber use fees. As described above, federal officials may charge such fees only if facilities meet legally defined standards. Moreover, Hoosier National Forest officials retain only 15 percent of the use fee revenue they collect, and that money must be spent on the facilities that generated it.

An interesting rule that does affect use fee collection on national forests relates to concessionaires. Concessionaires are private contractors who agree to provide services on federal land to earn revenue, in exchange for which they pay a portion of their revenues to the USDA Forest Service. They may pay their due in one of two forms: a monetary sum to the U.S. Treasury or in-kind goods or services of "equivalent value" to the local forest. Federal officials in Indiana prefer that the payments be made in-kind to their forest, rather than remitted to the "black hole" in the Treasury. Moreover, the concessionaires may believe that investing locally can increase their business. Thus, both parties have a strong incentive to see that the revenue sharing is through local improvements rather than a check to the U.S. Treasury. Federal officials on the forest work out agreements with concessionaires, as one official described:

> For example, we'll say, "If you provide X picnic tables, we'll consider
> it to be worth $Y." Perhaps the concessionaire can do it himself or get
> a favorable contract to complete the project for less than $Y. That way,
> he can benefit and the forest gets the additional picnic tables.

In fact, concessionaires operate all but one of the national forest campgrounds in Indiana. Officials would like to contract out this one exception as well, but the area has relatively low use and income potential, so no concessionaires have been willing to bid for the contract. Thus, in Indiana, federal officials have strong incentives to shift recreational service provision and fee collection to private contractors. Officials also regard such a shift as a viable strategy for keeping camping facilities open in the face of declining recreational line item allocations from Congress. However, federal officials, like state officials, do not face incentives to collect additional nontimber use fees.

Washington

The potential exists for Washington state forest officials to increase budgetary resources through use fee collection. A share of all use fees collected (25 percent for school trust lands and some county trust lands, 50 percent for other county trust lands) goes into the fund from which the legislature allocates the agency's budget. The incentive to increase use fee collection is diminished by liability concerns, however. As in Ohio and Indiana, state officials in Washington fear a greater risk of liability lawsuits for injured recreationists who have paid fees, which could substantially affect agency resources. State officials also question whether the share retained by the agency would cover the costs of collection. Hence, financial considerations limit the incentive for state officials to increase use fee collection.

Federal officials in Washington face similar restrictions on use fee collection to those of their counterparts on other national forests. Because only 15 percent of fees collected stay on Gifford Pinchot National Forest, there is little incentive to increase use fees. As on other national forests, concessionaire payment arrangements and limited agency recreation budget allocations provide an incentive to shift fee campground management to private concessionaires. Thus, officials have contracted out management of most campgrounds. There is no incentive, however, to increase user fee revenues as a means to enhance their budgets.

Oregon

In theory, Oregon state forest officials have an incentive to charge use fees as a way to increase budgetary resources. Fees collected accrue to the state agency headquarters, where the trust beneficiary share is paid (63.75 percent goes to counties, and 100 percent less management expenses goes to schools) and the rest is available for the agency to use, following authorization by the state legislature. In practice, financial considerations temper this incentive. Officials fear that, if fees are set too high, more users might avoid payment, necessitating expending greater agency resources for monitoring.

Federal officials in Oregon see a growing potential for generating revenue from use fees, especially for permits to collect commercially valuable special forest products such as floral greenery, mushrooms, and cedar boughs. They are frustrated, however, by the incentive structure that transfers 85 percent of such fees to the U.S. Treasury, rather than allowing them to stay on Siuslaw National Forest for development of the special forest product program. With a steadily declining recreation budget, staff members are constrained in their ability to increase recreational use fee collection, which generally requires more resources than are generated from the 15 percent of use fees that stays on the forest.

An interesting development regarding use fee collection on the Siuslaw National Forest involves an experimental program to alter the use fee revenue structure. In April 1996, Congress authorized a three-year pilot program that allowed participating federal agencies to develop new use fees and retain most of these new revenues for use at the site where they are collected (PL 104-34). This arrangement gives officials greater opportunities to gain and retain use fees to increase their budgets. Several federal officials described the new program as a helpful opportunity to fund popular recreation sites at higher levels. As one official said, "This is a good program—I think it represents the future of forest management here, where we are able to gain economic benefits from many nontimber resources." In fact, the fee program was extended in 1998, and a GAO report described positive results, with hundreds of millions of dollars raised from federal lands to be spent on improving recreational facilities. At the same time, several federal agency officials noted that spending limited to demonstration sites made charging recreational fees less desirable (GAO 1999).

Nontimber Use Fees Summary

Within the four forest pairs, nontimber use fee revenue structures in place in fiscal year 1995 did not provide substantial incentives for increasing use fee collection by state and federal officials. Although state agencies accrued a substantial portion of use fees collected to the agency headquarters, state officials were hesitant to increase nontimber use fee collection because of liability concerns and financial concerns relating to monitoring and collection costs. Similarly, federal officials did not regard raising nontimber use fees to be an effective means to increase revenue because of the costs of monitoring and collection and because of the revenue-sharing formula, which allowed them to retain only 15 percent of revenues on the forest where use fees were collected.

Timber Sales

Nontimber use fees related to recreation and special forest products account for a relatively small portion of revenue for the forest agencies. A more important potential revenue source is the sale of trees for timber to private contractors. In the forest pairs examined here, contrary to functional theory of federalism expectations, rules do not provide stronger revenue incentives for state officials to sell more timber than they do for federal officials.

Ohio

Ohio state forest officials do not retain any revenues from timber sales. Instead, all "stumpage" (the right to harvest a given set of standing trees) payments accrue to the state general fund. Interestingly, this rule for timber revenue accrual used to be different: In the 1980s the rule prescribed that the state forest agency would retain timber revenue to fund its own programs. Agency officials requested the change, however—negotiating a new rule whereby they would give up timber revenue in exchange for a higher biennial appropriation level. Agency officials who pushed for this change preferred the uncertainty of legislative appropriations to the uncertainty of fluctuating timber prices and harvests.[2]

Unlike state forest officials, federal officials in Ohio are entitled to retain a share of timber revenue for use on Wayne National Forest, through the Knutsen-Vandenberg Act (K-V Act). Thus, federal officials may have a direct incentive to increase timber provision. Moreover, the share of timber revenue retained is based on gross receipts rather than net profit, leading several scholars to argue that USDA Forest Service officials have an incentive to overharvest forests, selling timber at "below cost" prices to increase revenues for their budgets (see, for example, Budiansky 1991; O'Toole 1988; Rice 1989).

For the national forest in Ohio, however, such criticism is misplaced. Although the rules appear to provide a strong incentive to overharvest, in reality federal officials do not view the K-V Act as an important factor in timber sale decisions. Use of timber revenues on a given national forest is constrained by Forest Service regional limits. As one official explained,

> K-V funding is not a reason to have a sale. We do timber sales for forest health and ecosystem reasons, with K-V funding as a possible benefit, so long as the regional ceiling has not been reached. But if other forests are ahead of us in line for funding from the region, then we may not receive any such K-V funds.

Another federal official in Ohio noted that, because the use of K-V funds is limited to projects within the timber sale area, sometimes part of the funds to which the forest is otherwise entitled are unneeded and thus revert to the U.S. Treasury. For example, in one timber sale, officials budgeted only half of the allocated K-V funds for work in the timber sale area, returning the rest to the U.S. Treasury. Therefore, in Ohio, timber sales on the national forest do not provide the K-V windfall that some scholars have suggested.

Indiana

In Indiana, neither state nor federal officials face significant incentives to increase timber sales to enhance their budgets. On Indiana state forests, timber sales revenues accrue to a dedicated fund, but the agency must seek authority from the state legislature to spend these revenues. Neither local nor headquarters forest officials see a direct link between timber revenue and agency revenues. As one state official explained,

> The dedicated fund is not a revolving fund; we don't use in one year what was earned the previous year. Instead, dedicated fund money goes through the appropriations process, which I believe is good as a safeguard against short-term thinking, and it reduces our incentive to focus on maximizing revenue.

Similarly, federal officials in Indiana lack financial incentives to increase timber sales. On one hand, K-V funds may be made available as a result of timber sales. One official suggested that such revenue can be very useful for performing work in the sale area, such as wildlife openings, trail maintenance, and stocking surveys. On the other hand, timber sales on this forest tended to be relatively small, with correspondingly low K-V revenue. For example, the K-V revenue requested for one sale amounted to just $4,000—a trivial proportion (about 0.1 percent) of the agency's operating expenditures for managing public forest lands. A federal official noted,

> On this forest, K-V funds are not a significant enough amount of money to provide a reason to harvest more. The money is to be used for specific projects, like reforestation, TSI, or wildlife habitat in the sale area. You have to balance the extra funds with the need to provide the extra work. I've heard some critics say the foresters are doing sales to get K-V money, but I don't know anybody who's drumming up sales in order to increase K-V funds.

Washington

In Washington, state officials do not gain revenue directly from timber sales. Instead (as described in the appropriations discussion), a portion of timber sale revenue accrues to a dedicated fund, which agency officials may spend only after legislative authorization. Thus, the budget is only indirectly tied to timber sales. Although timber sales provide an important argument when the agency makes its budget request, the connection between increasing timber sales and receiving higher budget allocations is weak. One state official explained that, no matter what the argument, the agency expects that the legislature will not often allocate the budget amount requested by the agency.

Federal officials in Washington are entitled to keep certain revenues earned through timber sales. K-V funds are a useful by-product of timber sales for the federal agency; in fiscal year 1995, Gifford Pinchot National Forest received $0.9 million in K-V funding, which represented 5 percent of its total operating expenses for public forest land management. Moreover, federal officials use a revolving salvage sale fund, which includes revenue from salvage sales (trees that are diseased or dying or in imminent danger of becoming diseased or dying), to prepare additional salvage sales on the forest. In fiscal year 1995, officials on Gifford Pinchot National Forest collected $1.3 million in salvage sale revenues, which represented 7 percent of the agency's total operating expenses for public forest land management. Thus, timber sale revenues are directly tied to about 12 percent of the agency's operating expenditures. The significance of these revenues as an incentive is tempered, however, by other constraints that limit the amount of timber that officials prepare for sale. One national forest official explained, "We haven't increased sales to get more K-V funding. We do what's best for the land, working toward our 73 million board-feet target, which we haven't reached yet."

Oregon

In Oregon, as in Washington, state officials do not directly gain revenue from timber sales. Instead, budget allocations are made by the state legislature from timber sales and other agency revenues. Thus, the budget incentive to increase timber sales is indirect. State officials report, however, that authorizations are not a significant limiting factor because the agency usually is authorized to spend whatever it requests, as long as the resources are present in the forest management fund. One state official commented, "We have no problem getting legislative authorization. We've even gone back to ask for supplemental authorization and, as far as I can recall, we've never been turned down." Another state official concurred: "I usually get what I ask for in authorizations." Therefore, the incentive to increase timber sales is strong because officials expect to be able to use these earnings to fund agency expenditures.

Federal officials in Oregon have an incentive to sell more timber to increase the agency's budget. In fiscal year 1995, Siuslaw National Forest officials received $2.9 million in K-V funds and $0.3 million in salvage sale funds, which together totaled 23 percent of the agency's operating expenses for public forest land management. K-V and salvage revenues are not key determinants of timber sales, however, because the use of these earnings is limited to specific project work or additional salvage sales. One official explained, "K-V earnings are not a reason to put up more sales because we're limited by Plan targets and small number of staff."

Summary of Budget Incentives

With respect to budget, comparing state agency rules with federal agency rules does not support expectations from the functional theory of federalism. For the largest share of forest agency revenues—budget appropriations—state officials in Washington and Oregon, as well as federal officials in Washington, do regard increasing activities that generate timber as a useful budget strategy. This is not true of state officials in Ohio or Indiana, however. Thus, there appears to be a regional difference—with appropriations incentives encouraging timber in the region where timber is in higher quantities and more important to the regional economy—rather than a difference based on level of government. Moreover, throughout all of the forest pairs, officials indicate a generally low level of efficacy regarding their ability to influence budget allocations, no matter what their strategies.

Nor do nontimber user payments provide significant budget incentives. For state officials, the low proportion of agency revenue from nontimber use fees, combined with the drawbacks of use fee liabilities and collection costs or inability to affect use fee rates, dampen budget incentives that might otherwise promote activities with substantial, direct economic benefits. Similarly, nontimber use fees do not provide revenue incentives for federal officials, who are allowed to collect fees only under certain conditions and who face collection costs that easily exceed the 15 percent fee share that is retained.

With regard to timber sales, at the state level the accrual of stumpage receipts to the state treasury (Ohio) or to a dedicated fund subject to conservative legislative appropriations (Indiana and Washington) means that officials lack budget incentives for boosting timber sales. State officials in Oregon do have an incentive to increase timber sales, however, because sale earnings that accrue to a forest management fund generally are made available by the legislature for forest officials to spend. Federal officials, meanwhile, may earn revenue for the forest from timber sales through K-V funding or salvage sales. Across the national forests, however, officials described spending restrictions that limit the motivating power of this incentive in practice. Thus, budgetary incentives do not encourage state officials systematically to promote uses with direct economic benefits more than they encourage federal officials to do so.

Conclusion

Unlike the types of rules discussed in chapter 6, budget incentives do not exhibit systematic state-federal differences. Elected officials do not steer agency officials at the state level toward economic development through budget incentives. Nor do elected officials drive agency officials to increase noneconomic outputs at the federal level. Instead, the use of budgets to influence particular forest policy choices is attenuated by agency officials' perception that they are relatively powerless to affect their budgets through their behavior.

Interestingly, criticism that the K-V Act leads federal agency officials to increase timber harvest levels regardless of net profit is not supported in any of the four national forests. Although the K-V incentive may appear to be strong, in practice its influence is diminished by the existence of other forest management goals, as well as limits on funding retention and expenditure.

Further understanding of bureaucratic behavior requires an examination of three additional factors: citizens, agency officials' beliefs, and agency community. These factors are the focus of chapter 8.

Notes

1. The state legislators may face incentives to raise fees because increased user payments could be used to offset reduced spending from the state general fund. Indiana legislators have not pursued this action, however, perhaps fearing unhappy voters who would not welcome increased fees.

2. Loggers do not make stumpage payments until after they complete a harvest. A typical contract provides a two-year period in which the contractor must harvest and pay for the timber. When timber prices are low, many contractors choose to defer harvesting in hopes of higher prices later, which causes a downturn in state forest stumpage revenue in the current time period.

8 Beyond Elected Officials

In chapters 6 and 7, I describe the influence of rules on bureaucratic behavior. As created by elected officials, rules are one mechanism by which the functional theory of federalism can explain state-federal differences in agency policy. Evidence from the four forest pairs indicates that laws and forest plans do, indeed, favor agency pursuit of activities such as timber with direct, economic development more at the state level than at the federal level. On the other hand, budget incentives do not exhibit such systematic differences by level of government.

A fuller understanding of bureaucratic behavior requires an examination of not just rules but also sources of influence that do not originate from elected officials. Such factors, in fact, may be at odds with the wishes of elected officials—a point that has been debated by public administration scholars. For example, the Progressive Reform movement called for neutral bureaucrats with technical expertise to closely follow directives from elected officials. In practice, however, agency officials may have considerable autonomy from their political masters. Additional sources of influence include citizen pressure, agency officials' beliefs, and agency community. These factors are useful in accounting for the systematic state-federal differences in forest policy performance described in chapters 3 through 5. In particular, citizens wield dramatically different influence on federal policymaking than they do on state forest agency policymaking.

Citizen Pressure

A rich history of scholarship suggests that citizen pressure is an important determinant of bureaucratic policymaking. In environmental regulatory policy at the federal level, Hoberg (1992) finds that citizen pressure accounts for the rise of policies favoring environmental protection over business interests. In addition, he describes the critical role of citizens, empowered by new statutory tools, in changing public forest policy on national forests (Hoberg 1997). Scholz (1988) notes a similar relationship in workplace regulatory policy, as statutory provisions legitimating participation of local interests significantly influence bureaucratic behavior. Local interests also are important in determining USDA Forest Service forest plan decisions, as Sabatier, Loomis, and McCarthy (1995) argue.

A handful of studies suggest that there may be systematic state-federal differences with regard to which types of citizen interests are more influential. Citizens who favor commodity production such as timber are described as wielding greater influence on state elected officials, whereas environmental preservation interests are regarded as wielding greater influence on national elected officials.

Commodity Interests

According to the "iron triangle" or "cozy triangle" model of public policy at the federal level, executive agencies, congressional committees, and groups seeking economic payoffs tend to adopt mutual noninterference strategies of interaction (Parker 1989). The resulting policies favor economic interests over other interests. In the case of federal forest policy, the expectation is that timber interests prevail (see, for example, Barney 1974; Shepherd 1975). According to Souder and Fairfax (1996: 294), timber purchasers historically have dominated national forest management. Moreover, in a dissenting opinion in *Sierra Club v. Morton* (405 U.S. 727 [1972]), Justice Douglas argued that the USDA Forest Service was dominated by timber interests.

Scholars have argued, however, that the "iron triangle" that gives economic interests substantial power at the federal level was largely dismantled after 1970 as social regulation came to replace probusiness regulation in a variety of sectors (Hoberg 1992). Moreover, some researchers suggest that timber interests are even more influential at the state level. Davis (1993: 44) argues that higher-impact interests, especially those with large economic incentives to shape policy, exert greater influence at lower levels of government. Ziegler and van Dahlen (1976) also describe interest groups representing dominant economic interests as most influential at the state level. Furthermore, according to the functional theory of federalism, greater influence of economic interests at lower levels of government stems from greater mobility across states than nations; state elected officials fear repercussions (e.g., job losses, reduced tax base) from timber purchasers who may readily move operations out of state if state policies do not emphasize economic goals sufficiently (Peterson 1995). For the analysis here I examine whether this expectation is met in policy made by nonelected agency officials.

Preservation Interests

Several scholars have suggested that environmental groups are likely to be more influential at higher levels of government. Nash (1982) argues that support for natural resource protection is stronger among people who live far from the resource than among those who live near it. Several survey research efforts have supported this attitudinal difference (see Tremblay and Dunlap 1978; Lowe and Pinhey 1982). Similarly, Robinson (1975) states that preservation-oriented groups tend to be more successful at higher levels of government. One example is the northern spotted owl controversy in the Pacific Northwest; largely through the work of national environmental interest groups, such as the Audubon Society, the USDA Forest Service was forced to halt timber sales in federal old-growth forest that provided habitat for northern spotted owls. These results are in line with the functional theory of federalism, which argues that noneconomic interests are more likely to be pursued by federal elected officials than by state elected officials. Of course, in the analysis at hand, I am examining nonelected officials, so it remains to be tested whether federal agency personnel are influenced more by preservation interests than are state agency personnel.

State-Federal Differences in the Forest Pairs

As I indicate in chapter 6, federal agency officials face more stringent requirements to foster public participation than do state agency officials. Federal officials also face external actors armed with powerful tools—administrative appeals and lawsuits—to affect agency decisions. In contrast, state officials face fewer legal requirements to pursue public input, and opponents of state forest officials' activities have less legal power to block them. This contrast suggests differences in officials' interactions with citizens.

In chapter 5 I discuss differences in agency officials' efforts to foster citizen participation and the resulting differences in the frequency of communications with different citizen interest types. Recall that federal officials undertook greater efforts than did state officials to promote meaningful citizen participation in policymaking. Moreover, federal officials' communication patterns were dominated by preservation interests, whereas state officials communicated more with timber interests.

The findings in chapters 5 and 6 raise the question: Are patterns of citizen influence systematically different as well? My analysis reveals that citizens who favor preservation wield greater influence at the federal level, whereas those favoring timber provision wield greater influence at the state level.

Officials' Perceptions of Citizen Influence

To examine influence, I first measured officials' perceptions. Because citizens may influence agency policymaking through direct communication with agency officials as well as through their elected officials or legal challenges, I gathered data for three different channels of influence: (a) communicating with agency officials, (b) pressure on legislators, and (c) administrative or court challenges. A standard questionnaire item asked officials to indicate, on a scale of 1 (no influence) to 5 (very influential), the amount of influence of various types of citizens in affecting forest management, through each of the three channels (see Appendix A).

For citizens favoring preservation, mean influence scores differ as expected, across all three channels, and these differences are statisti-

Table 8.1. Mean Influence Scores, Officials' Perceptions of Citizen Influence

Interest Type	Federal Officials			State Officials			Diff. in Mean[b]
	Mean[a]	St. Dev.	N	Mean	St. Dev.	N	
Channel (a): Contacting Agency Personnel							
Timber	2.90	0.94	31	3.15	0.83	33	–0.25
Preservation	3.10	0.83	31	2.75	1.05	32	0.35[c]
Channel (b): Pressure on Legislators							
Timber	3.16	1.21	31	2.94	1.01	32	0.22
Preservation	3.32	0.98	31	2.78	1.26	32	0.54[d]
Channel (c): Administrative Appeals or Court Challenges							
Timber	2.84	1.13	31	2.94	1.25	33	–0.10
Preservation	3.32	1.08	31	2.72	1.30	32	0.60[d]

[a]Values are integers from 1 (no influence) to 5 (high influence).
[b]Positive values indicate higher federal mean; negative values indicate higher state mean.
[c]Significant at 0.10 level.
[d]Significant at 0.05 level.

cally significant (see Table 8.1).[1] Moreover, mean influence scores differ in the opposite direction for citizens favoring timber, in channels (a) and (c), although these differences are not statistically significant.

Citizen Participants' Perceptions of Their Influence

To explore influence further, I asked citizen participants to indicate whether their actions were more likely to have an impact on policies of the state or federal agency. Although some participants were not able to make such a comparison because of limited involvement with one or the other agency, others did indicate their perceptions about influence. As shown in Table 8.2, those favoring timber perceived greater influence on state forests, whereas those favoring preservation perceived greater influence on national forests.

In Ohio, three of four respondents favoring preservation who attempted to influence both agencies perceived greater influence in federal policy, compared to none in state policy. In contrast, no timber

Table 8.2. Citizen Participants' Perceived Influence

| Interest Type | No. of Citizens Perceiving More Influence with the Following Agency | | | |
	Total	Federal	State	Equal
Ohio				
Preservation	4	3	0	1
Timber	2	0	1	1
Indiana				
Preservation	8	6	1	1
Timber	5	0	3	2
Washington				
Preservation	1	1	0	0
Timber	5	0	4	1
Oregon				
Preservation	4	4	0	0
Timber	3	0	3	0
Total, Preservation	17	14	1	2
Total, Timber	15	0	11	4

advocate who attempted to influence both agencies perceived greater influence in federal policy, compared to one of two in state policy.

In Indiana, six of eight individuals favoring preservation who attempted to influence both agencies perceived greater influence on the national forest, and only one perceived greater influence on the state forests. Conversely, among timber advocates who attempted to influence both agencies, none perceived greater influence on federal forest policies, compared to three of five who perceived greater influence on state forest policies.

In Washington, the only preservation-oriented individual who dealt with both agencies described greater influence on the national forest than on state forests. In contrast, no timber advocate who attempted to influence both agencies indicated greater influence on national forests, and four of five indicated greater influence on state forests.

In Oregon, all four individuals favoring preservation who attempted to influence both agencies described greater influence on the national forest than on state forests. In contrast, all three individuals favoring timber who attempted to influence both agencies indicated greater influence on state forests.

Overall, fourteen of seventeen preservation proponents perceived greater influence on national forests, and only one perceived greater influence on state forests. Conversely, no timber proponent perceived greater influence on national forests, whereas eleven of fifteen perceived greater influence on state forests. Thus, evidence from the four forest pairs suggests important differences in citizen participants' perceptions of influence. Those favoring preservation perceived greater influence in federal than state agency policies, whereas those favoring timber perceived greater influence in state than federal agency policies.

Forest Agency Officials' Beliefs

Scholars have recognized the role of agency officials' beliefs[2] in shaping their policymaking behavior. As one forest policy study claims, "Values are central to understanding people and their relationships to their environments and equally important to understanding organizations such as the U.S. Forest Service" (Cramer et al. 1993: 479). Also at the federal level, Eisner and Meier (1990) found that agency members' norms and attitudes were more important than presidential or congressional directives in changing the Department of Justice's antitrust policies. More generally, Meier (1993) describes the substantial impacts bureaucratic beliefs can have on federal policy implementation. At the state level, Rabe (1986) highlights the importance of state agency officials' beliefs in developing permitting innovations. Likewise, Ringquist (1990) notes the role of agency officials' preferences in implementing state air quality regulations.

Substantively, in examining what beliefs agency officials hold, researchers have emphasized federal personnel. In the forest sector, USDA Forest Service employees have been portrayed as holding narrowly timber-oriented beliefs. Scholars commonly have attributed this set of values to organizational culture as well as to individuals' educational background and identification with local communities. For example, Kaufman (1960) describes employee recruitment, training, and relocation that encouraged adherence to the agency's dominant paradigm of forest management for commodity production—principally timber. Similarly, Twight and Lyden (1988) and O'Toole (1988) describe USDA Forest Service officials as holding predominantly timber-oriented beliefs. More recently, however, studies of Forest Service employees' values and behavior indicate that they are becoming less narrowly timber-oriented, siding more often with environmental and recreational interests (Brown and Harris 2000; Cramer et al. 1993; Tipple and Wellman 1991).

Analysts have undertaken much less research to understand employees in state forest agencies, to test the longstanding view that better-educated, more capable individuals who are interested in public service are attracted to federal rather than state government because of better pay and civil service protection (White 1953: 63). More recently, state employees have exhibited increased professionalism and capacity to meet policy challenges (Cigler 1993; Bowman and Kearney 1986; Eisinger 1988). A common disciplinary background in forestry and professional organizations such as the Society of American Foresters may link individuals across forest agencies at different governmental levels (Thompson and Scicchitano 1985). Thus, state forest officials may model their behavior on, and hold beliefs similar to, USDA Forest Service officials (Souder and Fairfax 1996: 245).

To compare state officials' beliefs with federal officials' beliefs across the forest pairs, I used a written survey. Forest officials completed a confidential questionnaire that asked them to indicate the response that most closely matched their beliefs about a variety of forest management statements (see Appendix A). Responses for each statement were arrayed on a 5-point scale, labeled "strongly favor," "favor," "neither favor nor disfavor," "disfavor," and "strongly disfavor." Each completed response is coded as 2 (strongly favor), 1 (favor), 0 (neither), –1 (disfavor), or –2 (strongly disfavor).

Table 8.3 displays questionnaire results. First, note that mean scores vary across questionnaire items. For example, officials at state and federal agencies tend to disfavor increasing oil/gas/mineral extraction and off-road vehicle (ORV) trails, yet they strongly favor charging recreational use fees and increasing efforts to seek public input. Second, comparing across agencies, it is apparent that federal response means are higher in a majority of the pairs. For most items, however, the response value difference is trivial; federal and state official mean values differ by less than 0.50 for eleven of the fourteen items.

Table 8.3. Mean Response Values from Officials' Questionnaires

| | State Officials | | | Federal Officials | | | Diff. in |
Questionnaire Item	Mean[a]	s.d.	N	Mean	s.d.	N	Mean[b]
Managing with ecosystem focus	0.62	0.99	39	0.78	0.90	36	-.16
Increasing horse trails	0.13	1.01	39	0.26	1.01	35	-.13
Increasing hiking trails	0.56	0.85	39	0.97	0.75	35	-.41[c]
Increasing oil/gas/ mineral extraction	-.51	0.89	39	-.43	0.82	35	-.08
Increasing timber	0.44	1.02	39	0.17	0.85	36	0.27
Increasing hunting/ fishing	0.58	0.78	40	0.60	0.70	35	-.02
Favoring local economic development	0.53	0.79	40	0.50	0.70	36	0.03
Charging recreational use fees	0.60	0.90	40	1.20	0.72	35	-.12
Increasing public input	0.90	0.93	40	1.11	0.85	36	-.21
Increasing developed camping	-.21	0.95	39	0.31	1.05	35	-.52
Increasing ORV trails	-.77	1.09	39	-.56	1.11	36	-.21
Active conversion to native species	0.71	0.90	38	0.94	0.89	36	-.23
Increasing wilderness/ preservation	0.03	1.27	39	0.36	0.99	36	-.33
Allowing clearcutting	1.48	0.60	40	0.42	1.30	36	1.06[d]

[a]Values range from -2 (strongly disfavor) to 2 (strongly favor).
[b]Positive values indicate higher state mean; negative values indicate higher federal mean.
[c]Significant at 0.05 level.
[d]Significant at 0.01 level.

Statistical tests confirm that state and federal officials' responses do not differ systematically across the items. As indicated in Table 8.3, state and federal officials' response values are significantly different (at the 0.05 level of significance) for only two questionnaire items: increasing hiking trails and allowing clearcutting.[3] Although differences in these two items indicate more favorable attitudes among federal officials toward one noneconomic benefit and among state officials for one activity that promotes economic development, it is important to note that the responses on the remaining twelve items are not significantly different.

These results reveal that officials' beliefs do not exhibit systematic differences across levels of governance. This finding is important because it indicates that the policy performance differences described in chapters 3 through 5 are not a result of differences in officials' beliefs.

Agency Community

The third factor that is described as influential in agency officials' behavior involves attributes of the community in which they work. Socially constructed understanding among members of an organization can powerfully influence their behavior (Ott 1989; Shafritz and Russell 1997). For example, in one federal-level study, the researcher concludes that organizational culture played a central role in shaping bureaucratic behavior in the Bureau of Prisons (DiIulio 1994).

Important community attributes include shared norms and homogeneity (Ostrom, Gardner, and Walker 1994). Agencies with a wide variety of job positions face challenges in developing a cohesive community with shared norms and beliefs. On the other hand, agencies with long employment tenures and high levels of relocation may be well positioned to breed a culture of conformity among members, as new members initially seek to fit in (Kaufman 1960).

Across the forest pairs, I measure agency community by three indicators: rates of employee turnover and relocation, job position variety, and homogeneity of officials' beliefs. Although federal-state differences are evident in the first two indicators, they are not evident in the third.

Employee Turnover and Relocation

Overall, federal forest officials tend to have longer employment tenures with their agency than do their state counterparts. Across the forest pairs, federal officials I interviewed had spent an average 18.6 years with their agency, whereas state officials had spent an average

Table 8.4. Officials' Length of Employment with Agency

Agency	No. of Respondents	No. of Years with Agency		
		Longest	Shortest	Mean
Ohio				
Federal	10	29	5	17.1
State	10	22	6	15.6
Indiana				
Federal	10	20	5	15.4
State	9	24	6	16.1
Washington				
Federal	11	32	10	20.9
State	11	26	3	13.8
Oregon				
Federal	11	28	7	20.7
State	14	24	1	12.2
Total, Federal	42	32	5	18.6
Total, State	44	26	1	13.8

13.8 years with their agency (see Table 8.4). This difference is statistically significant at the 0.01 level.[4]

In addition to employment tenure, it is important to investigate officials' job mobility within each organization. Across the forest pairs, federal agency officials indicated greater mobility—as measured by the number of years working for the agency divided by the number of locations served—than did state agency officials. The mean time spent per location for federal officials I interviewed was 5.1 years, compared to 7.2 years for state officials (see Table 8.5). This difference is statistically significant at the 0.01 level.[5]

Indeed, geographic mobility is critical to career success for federal officials. As one USDA Forest Service official in Ohio explained, "I wouldn't have been able to advance my career without having traveled to gain diverse work experiences." Another said, "It's rare for someone to be promoted in place." One federal official in Indiana said, "For promotions, being mobile is important, since you have to go where the jobs are." Another explained, "As I've moved up the ladder I've had to transfer locations—to move up you've got to move on." Similarly,

Table 8.5. Officials' Geographic Mobility within Organization

Agency	No. of Respondents	Average No. of Years per Location for an Employee		
		Longest	Shortest	Mean
Ohio				
Federal	10	6.0	2.4	3.7
State	10	16.0	5.0	7.6
Indiana				
Federal	10	9.5	2.5	5.5
State	9	13.0	4.3	8.2
Washington				
Federal	11	11.5	3.3	5.6
State	11	14.0	3.0	7.2
Oregon				
Federal	11	18.0	2.5	5.6
State	14	10.0	0.7	6.2
Total, Federal	42	18.0	2.4	5.1
Total, State	44	16.0	0.7	7.2

a federal official in Oregon said that without mobility, she would not have been able to advance as rapidly as she has.

Although such mobility can be useful in providing employees with a wealth of experience and increased loyalty to the organization, it can hinder the organization's ability to get work done when an employee leaves. For example, in one instance a vacant position in the federal agency in Ohio could not be filled until the start of the next fiscal year because the budget had no money available for the moving expense required to put a new hire into position. Furthermore, one federal official stated, "Turnover [from relocation] can cause problems in terms of knowing the local community and the forest; some local people complain that just when you get to know a Forest Service employee, he leaves."

At the state level, there are fewer incentives for mobility. One Ohio state official was content to continue in his current (mid-level) position, which he had held for more than five years, because any career advancement would require the hassle of relocating to a different city without a significant increase in pay. Although less mobility can promote personnel stability, it carries an organizational drawback in that people may develop "tunnel vision" rather than a broader range of experience that would be helpful in managing forest resources for multiple uses and users.

In addition to less time spent at each location, USDA Forest Service officials' geographic mobility often includes relocation across thousands of miles within the national forest system. For example, one Wayne National Forest official had worked for the Forest Service in Oregon, West Virginia, and North Carolina before coming to Ohio, and another previously had been assigned to forests in Colorado and California. In Indiana, Hoosier National Forest officials' past work locations included Alabama, Utah, South Carolina, and Oregon. One Gifford Pinchot National Forest official reported prior positions in Texas, Puerto Rico, Alaska, and North Carolina before his Washington location. In contrast, state employees who change locations within their organizations do so within a much smaller geographic range, limited to one state.

As noted above, federal officials exhibit greater length of employment in their organization and geographic mobility than do state officials. These work experiences are important for understanding officials' beliefs because officials who remain in an organization for a long period and relocate often are more likely to share common views about their profession and goals (Kaufman 1960).

Job Position Variety

Another important element of an agency community is the variety of job positions included. A greater diversity of views is more likely to come from an agency with a wider range of specialists. Compared to the state agency, the federal agency in each forest pair includes more positions that focus on nontimber aspects of forest management.

In Ohio, the federal agency includes two public and legislative affairs specialists, three planning and information management specialists, five engineers, eight lands/minerals/special uses specialists, six ecosystem specialists, two wildlife biologists, one botanist, one fisheries biologist, one (part-time) soil scientist, eight recreation specialists, one archaeologist, and one realty specialist. In contrast, the public forest management section of the state forest agency includes few officials dedicated to such specialized functions: One legislative affairs and two information and education specialists are shared with other sections, and there are no agency engineers, wildlife biologists, botanists, fisheries biologists, soil scientists, recreation specialists, or archaeologists.

The range of job positions in the state and federal forest agencies also differs in Indiana. The federal agency includes a wide variety of specialists, including positions in land management planning and public and legislative affairs, as well as soil science, civil engineering, botany, landscape architecture, archaeology, wildlife biology, and silviculture. In contrast, the state agency does not include such specialists. As one state official explained,

> We don't have any biologists, botanists, or ecologists on staff. We're more generalists, with resource positions responsible for several different resources. If we need expertise in certain areas, we have access to people in other divisions of the [natural resources] department, such as fish and wildlife or nature preserves.

In the state of Washington as well, the federal forest agency has a broader range of positions than does the state forest agency. The Gifford Pinchot National Forest staff includes several professionals in wildlife biology, botany, ecology, soil science, hydrology, silviculture, fisheries, geology, archaeology, landscape architecture, engineering, public affairs, timber sale administration, and recreation, among other specialties. Positions on the Washington state forest staff are primarily in silviculture and timber sale administration, with a handful of others in planning/inventory and landscape architecture, plus a public information officer. Although the staff includes several scientists, most are in "natural resource" science rather than more specialized fields. In fact, the agency includes just one full-time wildlife biologist, and there are no archaeologists, botanists, or ecologists on staff.

The Oregon forest pair exhibits a similar difference in the range of agency positions. As in other national forests, the Siuslaw National Forest staff includes specialists in public affairs, rural development, special events, NEPA, economics, geographical information systems (GIS), recreation, archaeology, timber, minerals, soil science, ecology, biology, and botany. The Oregon state forest staff includes fewer specialists, instead depending on other state agencies to provide expertise in a variety of fields. One state employee who had worked previously in the USDA Forest Service explained the difference as follows:

> The Forest Service has expertise such as soil scientists, biologists, and hydrologists on staff, while our agency has fewer specialists. Yes, we can work with staff from the state fish and wildlife agency, but it takes more time to get hold of them, and it's harder to get their time for our projects. For example, on two occasions I've tried to get soil scientists from the state agency to help, but instead I had to go outside to the national Natural Resource Conservation Service, which slowed my work.

Clearly, the federal agency community includes greater job position diversity than does the state agency community in each pair. Does this higher job position diversity lead to a community of members with vastly different beliefs about how to manage forests? Or do longer job tenure and more frequent relocations homogenize officials' beliefs?

Homogeneity of Officials' Beliefs

Questionnaire results provide a means to compare state agency homogeneity of beliefs among members with federal agency homogeneity of beliefs. Levels of homogeneity among officials of each agency are indicated by the distribution of officials' responses to questionnaire items (see Appendix A). Standard deviation values, which measure how dispersed the individual values are about the mean value for a particular agency, suggest similar levels of homogeneity among state and federal officials on most of the fourteen questionnaire items (see Tables 8.6 and 8.7).[6]

Table 8.6 shows that in Ohio, federal officials' standard deviation is greater than state officials' standard deviation for six of the fourteen questionnaire items. In Indiana, federal officials' standard deviation is greater for seven of the fourteen questionnaire items. Similarly, in Table 8.7, we see that federal officials' standard deviation is greater for five of the fourteen items in Washington and seven of the fourteen items in Oregon. In total, federal officials' standard deviation is greater in twenty-five of fifty-six comparisons, whereas state officials' standard

Table 8.6. Within-Agency Variance among Officials' Responses, Ohio and Indiana

| | Standard Deviation Values[a] | | | | | |
| | Ohio | | | Indiana | | |
Questionnaire Item	State	Fed.	**Diff.**	State	Fed.	**Diff.**
Managing with ecosystem focus	0.831	0.951	**−0.12**	0.866	1.389	**−0.52**
Increasing horse riding	0.924	0.535	**0.39**	1.093	0.707	**0.39**
Increasing hiking	1.206	1.366	**−0.16**	0.866	0.835	**0.03**
Increasing oil/gas/ minerals	0.820	0.756	**0.06**	0.866	1.035	**−0.17**
Increasing timber	0.843	0.983	**−0.14**	0.500	0.744	**−0.24**
Increasing hunting/ fishing	0.874	1.113	**−0.24**	1.054	0.886	**0.17**
Favoring local economic development	1.036	0.690	**0.35**	1.014	1.165	**−0.15**
Charging recreation use fees	0.934	0.632	**0.30**	1.000	1.188	**−0.19**
Increasing public input	0.924	0.894	**0.03**	0.928	1.188	**−0.26**
Increasing developed camping	0.505	0.488	**0.02**	0.882	0.518	**0.36**
Increasing ORV riding	0.874	0.900	**−0.03**	0.866	0.835	**0.03**
Active convert to native species	0.647	0.632	**0.01**	0.972	0.641	**0.33**
Increasing wilderness	0.874	0.577	**0.30**	0.726	0.744	**−0.02**
Allowing clearcutting	0.522	0.787	**−0.26**	1.000	0.744	**0.26**

[a]Values based on distribution about mean, which ranges from −2 (strongly disfavor) to 2 (strongly favor); larger standard deviation values indicate less homogeneity of beliefs on that item among members of the agency.

deviation is greater in thirty-one of fifty-six. Across the four pairs, in no instance is the standard deviation difference more than 1, and it is more than 0.5 only three times out of fifty-six comparisons. Moreover, the difference is less than 0.25 for a majority of the comparisons (thirty-seven of fifty-six).

These results do not suggest that homogeneity of beliefs differs systematically between state and federal agencies. Despite the wider variety of job positions in federal agencies, federal officials do not exhibit greater heterogeneity. On the other hand, federal officials' higher lev-

Table 8.7. Within-Agency Variance among Officials' Responses,
Washington and Oregon

| | Standard Deviation Values[a] | | | | | |
| | Washington | | | Oregon | | |
Questionnaire Item	State	Fed.	**Diff.**	State	Fed.	**Diff.**
Managing with ecosystem focus	0.756	0.874	**–0.12**	0.452	1.160	**–0.71**
Increasing horse riding	0.756	0.751	**0.01**	1.775	0.850	**0.93**
Increasing hiking	0.756	0.751	**0.01**	0.651	1.033	**–0.38**
Increasing oil/gas/ minerals	1.380	0.944	**0.44**	1.293	1.247	**0.05**
Increasing timber	0.535	0.751	**–0.22**	0.835	0.667	**0.17**
Increasing hunting/ fishing	0.816	0.809	**0.01**	1.055	1.075	**–0.02**
Favoring local economic development	0.835	1.751	**0.08**	1.084	0.632	**0.45**
Charging recreation use fees	0.976	1.079	**–0.10**	0.751	0.876	**–0.12**
Increasing public input	0.991	0.751	**0.24**	0.669	0.632	**0.04**
Increasing developed camping	0.916	0.820	**0.10**	0.905	0.675	**0.23**
Increasing ORV riding	0.835	0.786	**0.05**	0.900	0.516	**0.38**
Active convert to native species	0.707	0.809	**–0.10**	0.900	1.033	**–0.13**
Increasing wilderness	0.690	0.505	**0.19**	0.900	1.160	**–0.26**
Allowing clearcutting	0.690	0.701	**–0.01**	0.492	0.516	**–0.02**

[a]Values based on distribution about mean, which ranges from –2 (strongly disfavor) to 2 (strongly favor); larger standard deviation values indicate less homogeneity of beliefs on that item among members of the agency.

els of job mobility and greater length of tenure do not lead to greater levels of homogeneity in their beliefs. Thus, the policy performance differences in chapters 3 through 5 are not caused by state-federal differences in homogeneity of the agency community.

Conclusion

Bureaucratic behavior theories point to several factors beyond elected officials that shape agency officials' policy choices. The analysis in this chapter has examined three such factors: citizens, agency officials' beliefs, and agency community.

Analysis of citizen influence reveals systematic differences in whose interests are favored at different levels of governance. As Peterson (1981) and Heclo (1978) have argued, nonbusiness interests perceive greater influence at higher levels of governance. Such perceptions of differences in influence are reflected in Sagebrush Rebellion proponents, as described in chapter 1, who demanded devolution of policy authority from federal to state agencies to increase their ability to press for economic development of forests and range lands. More recently, many of the calls for devolution of public forests from federal to state control come from those with an interest in using forests for higher levels of economic development.

In terms of influence, citizen participants favoring preservation perceive that they are more influential in federal forest policy than state forest policy, whereas citizen participants favoring timber perceive that they are more influential in state forest policy than federal forest policy. Agency officials, who traditionally have been trained to be neutral experts, do not perceive such a systematic difference in the influence of citizens favoring timber, although they do perceive that preservation proponents are more influential at the federal level.

In contrast to citizens' influence, I found no systematic differences in agency officials' beliefs. Quantitative analysis reveals that, for most questionnaire items (twelve of fourteen), state and federal officials do not significantly differ in their beliefs about appropriate forest management. This finding means that explanation of state-federal differences in agency policy performance rests on other factors.

Finally, I found that agency community characteristics differ systematically in some respects. Federal officials exhibit significantly higher levels of employee relocation as well as tenure within their agency. These characteristics fit with the traditional emphasis in the USDA Forest Service on high geographic mobility as well as promotion from within, which increased the homogeneity of beliefs within the agency. At the same time, however, the Forest Service exhibits a substantially higher level of job position variety—a characteristic that can increase the heterogeneity of beliefs in the agency community. These opposing characteristics appear to neutralize each other; the

level of homogeneity of beliefs, as measured by the beliefs' questionnaire, is remarkably similar across levels of government.

Citizens, agency officials' beliefs, and agency community are important pieces of the puzzle of differences in policy performance between state and federal forest agencies. After all, the functional theory
of federalism can explain state-federal–level differences in policymaking by elected officials, but it does not address agency policymaking. The analysis described in this chapter points to citizen influence, along with agency job mobility, tenure, and job position diversity,
as factors that may contribute to the systematic differences in agency
policy performance described in chapters 3 through 5. In chapter 9,
I combine these factors with the rules I examined in chapters 6 and 7
to more fully explain state-federal differences.

Notes

1. Statistical testing used two-sample t-test procedures. T-values and corresponding p-values were calculated for a one-tailed test.

2. Here *beliefs* refer to an individual's views about how forests ought to be managed—from a technical perspective as well as normatively—including attitudes, values, and preferences.

3. Response values for the first seven items exhibit a normal distribution; that is,
more responses from state and national officials fall toward the center of the –2 to 2
range, and fewer responses are toward the outside of the range. A pooled t-test is
appropriate for these normally distributed responses. For the remaining seven questionnaire items, response values do not exhibit a normal distribution. For example,
officials across each agency disfavor increasing ORV trails; the most frequent response
values are –2 and –1. A nonparametric test (Kolmogorov-Smirnov) provides statistical evidence for the items with responses that are not normally distributed. See Appendix B for a more thorough description of the statistical tests.

4. See Appendix B for a more thorough description of the statistical tests.

5. Ibid.

6. Statistical tests for differences in standard deviations between two samples are
not robust for small samples, especially those that are not normally distributed. Therefore, statistical tests are not included.

Part Four

Theoretical and Practical Implications

9 Explaining Policy Performance Differences

As described in chapters 6 through 8, bureaucratic behavior theory suggests four types of factors that are likely to influence agency policymaking: rules, citizens, agency officials' beliefs, and agency community. Analysis of these factors provides a basis for explaining the state-federal agency policy performance differences discussed in chapters 3 through 5. In particular, several of these factors account for differences in timber, profits, and revenue sharing; environmental protection; and citizen participation in policy processes.

Timber, Profits, and Revenue Sharing

Systematic differences between state and federal forest policy are evident in timber sales, profitability, and revenue sharing. Recall that state agency officials provide substantially higher timber volumes than do their federal counterparts. The greater emphasis on timber also is reflected in state agencies devoting a higher portion of agency operating expenditures to timber provision. Profitability also differs systematically; state agencies generate higher economic profits from timber provision than do federal agencies. Finally, state agencies provide larger transfer payments to local governments. These differences can be attributed primarily to rules and to citizen participation and influence.

Timber Sales

A key factor explaining federal agencies' relatively low volume of timber sales is the set of rules shaping officials' behavior. The first important rule is the requirement, through the NFMA and its implementing regulations, for officials to conduct extensive presale activities on national forests. In 1995, federal officials in Ohio, Indiana, and Oregon sold timber primarily from one district on the forest, after completing extensive interdisciplinary planning and analysis for the area. Reduced congressional budgets limited federal officials' ability to hire additional employees to perform more of the required timber sale preparation work. As one federal official explained, "We don't have enough personnel to focus on sales in more than one area per year." Presale requirements reduced the acreage from which timber sales could be completed.

A second critical legal constraint affecting timber provision is laws granting citizens the power to block harvesting. Citizens who oppose timber sales on public forests can more easily delay or stop such sales on the national forest than on state forests, using administrative appeals or legal challenges provided through the NFMA and NEPA (see chapter 6). For example, one Wayne National Forest official said that an environmental group was committed to appealing every timber sale on the national forest. In Indiana, opponents appealed all three national forest timber sales offered between 1991 and 1995, and in Washington, federal officials faced more than 30 appeals during fiscal year 1995 alone on the Gifford Pinchot National Forest. In contrast, state officials did not face opponents with such potent legal hammers.

In addition, patterns of communication affect timber sales. Interactions with citizens are linked to higher timber volumes sold on the state forests compared to the national forests. State officials tended to interact with many people who supported increased timber sales. For example, the hand delivery of Ohio state forest revenue-sharing checks to local government officials enhanced a close tie between the state official and the funding recipients. As one state official recognized, "Revenue that the agency earns and shares is very important to counties and townships in this region—the local money has a multiplier effect." Recall also that nearly every timber proponent inter-viewed in each forest pair reported more communication with state officials than with federal officials (see chapter 5). Consequently, tim-ber proponents perceived greater influence at the state level than at the federal level (see chapter 8). I explain these differences in citizen participation and influence in the third section of this chapter.

Timber Profitability

Why did state and federal unit profits on timber differ so sharply? This question is best answered by examining the cost and revenue com-ponents of timber provision. On the cost side, higher federal expenses reflect three key factors: planning constraints, appeals processes, and economies of scale.

First, as discussed in chapter 6, federal officials must comply with a greater number of legal constraints affecting timber management, which require greater agency resources. For example, officials nor-mally offer timber sales only after completing a thorough interdisci-plinary environmental assessment and landscape-level analysis of the area in which the trees are located. Officials charge the cost of such planning, which is required by the NFMA, to timber growth man-agement and sale administration accounts.

Second, federal officials face substantial costs in addressing timber sales appeals, as provided under NEPA and NFMA. Officials include expenses related to timber sale appeals in calculating timber costs.

Third, timber provision exhibits significant economies of scale. Costs associated with sale design, setup, bid processing, and compli-ance monitoring are substantial even for small timber sales, where they contribute to high unit costs. Relatively low timber sale volumes exhibit higher unit costs to provide, which lowers unit profitability. In each forest pair, the federal agency sold a lower volume of timber than did the state agency (see chapter 3).

On the revenue side, timber unit revenue is lower on national forests than on state forests across all four pairs. The lower unit rev-enues that federal agencies earn reflect several factors. A primary fac-tor involves rules described in chapter 6. Buyers may be hesitant to purchase timber on national forests because they are aware that avenues for appeal, as granted by NEPA and NFMA, can delay harvest operations. In fact, a tactic of one environmental group in Indiana that opposes timber sales on national forests has been to tell potential timber buyers that they will challenge harvesting activities. A member of the group described holding a rally to confront potential bidders: "We feel it is only fair that the bidders understand the full cost they will incur by buying these trees; these logging proposals will be challenged in every way possible."

A second reason for lower timber revenue on national forests is the tree species offered for sale. As described in chapter 2, in each of the four forest pairs, the state and national forests have a similar mix of tree species present. Officials may choose, however, to sell different species types. This happened in Indiana, where state forest officials sold predominantly hardwoods such as oak, poplar, and beech, but Hoosier National Forest officials sold only pine trees, a softwood species with lower commercial value. As one federal official explained,

> The Forest Plan intent was to focus on hardwood harvesting, but so far we've only sold pine. We've focused on this softwood because it's not native, so it's somewhat more acceptable to those who oppose harvesting on the forest. . . . Hardwoods are a different bag—selling them is likely to generate more controversy.

Thus, with NEPA and NFMA providing avenues for opponents to delay or block sales, federal officials in Indiana did not choose to sell hardwoods, which have higher commercial value but also higher probability of their sale being delayed by environmentalists using legal avenues.

A third reason for lower revenue per unit volume of timber on national forests relates to differing agency mandates, as described in chapter 6. Recall that state statutes direct state agencies to pursue profitable growth of timber (Ohio) and activities that generate revenue (Indiana, Washington, and Oregon). At the federal level, however, the Multiple-Use, Sustained-Yield Act (MUSYA) mandates that forests are not to be managed for maximum fiscal returns. Thus, timber sale objectives on national forests are less likely to focus on generating revenue or net profit than are objectives on state forests. Instead, federal officials often refer to timber sales as a "tool" to achieve other management goals, such as improving forest health or creating habitat for certain wildlife species.

A fourth reason for lower revenue per unit volume of timber on national forests is that federal officials face greater constraints on the type of harvesting techniques allowed. Limits on regeneration harvesting on national forests, as stipulated by the NFMA and in planning documents, can affect revenue. Instead of providing timber for harvest in large regeneration openings, federal officials must sell more timber for harvest by "thinning," which generally removes fewer large trees than does regeneration harvesting. Large trees typically have higher commercial value per board-foot than do small trees. As one federal official explained, "Typically we sell thinning harvests, featuring smaller logs with lower unit value—about $300 per thousand board-feet. In contrast, bigger trees can bring over $600 per thousand board-feet."

Finally, as the volume of timber sold dropped on the national forests in the Northwest, local mills went out of business or switched their settings to process timber from alternative sources—such as private lands, which included different tree species and log sizes. The resulting decrease in demand meant fewer bidders, with subsequently lowered bid values for national forest timber sales.

In summary, several factors combined to reduce unit revenues for timber sold on national forests compared with that sold on state forests. Contractors were likely to value national forest timber sales less than state timber sales if they foresaw risks of having their operations halted by citizen appeals. Moreover, some federal officials who were eager to avoid public controversy and timber sale blockages through appeals chose to sell less controversial—but less valuable— tree species. Differing statutory mandates directed forest management for different purposes; federal officials more often described timber sales as a tool for achieving other resource goals, whereas state officials were directed to pursue timber sales to generate revenue and profit. Another constraint affecting federal officials was harvest methods; the NFMA and planning documents restricted regeneration harvesting to a greater degree on national forests, resulting in the sale of smaller trees with lower market values. Finally, as timber sales volumes dropped in the Pacific Northwest, certain mills closed or converted to process logs from different sources, which reduced the number of bidders and, consequently, stumpage prices.

Revenue Sharing

It may be surprising that the state agency in each pair transferred more funds to local governments than did the federal agency. After all, in Ohio and Indiana, state revenue sharing was based on net rather than gross earnings, whereas federal revenue sharing was based on gross earnings (see chapter 3). Moreover, a narrower range of revenue sources was subject to sharing from the state than from the federal agency. Given these differences, we might expect state agencies to transfer smaller sums to local governments than do federal agencies.

In all four forest pairs, however, the state agency transferred more funds than did the federal agency. The critical factor determining this outcome is the higher level of revenue-generating activities, primarily timber, on state forests that provided a higher revenue base to which revenue-sharing formulas were applied.

Environmental Protection

Environmental protection as a policy output is an important measure of performance in natural resource policy. As described in chapter 5, federal officials undertook higher levels of efforts directed at environmental protection than did state officials across the four forest pairs. Such efforts were indicated by ecosystem-level management, rare species identification and protection, ecosystem research and monitoring, and soil and watershed protection and improvement. State-federal differences in environmental protection performance are attributable primarily to rules, as well as citizen influence.

Several rules are important in fostering greater environmental protection efforts at the federal level. First, unlike the state agencies, the federal agency's legal mandate does not place high priority on forest management for economic returns. Instead it emphasizes multiple uses, including wilderness and soil protection, equally.

Second, laws such as the NFMA and NEPA require interdisciplinary analysis of a wide range of resources, not just timber. Specifically, the NFMA and its implementing regulations constrain federal agency officials' timber harvesting techniques and harvest levels, and they require officials to protect species diversity. These laws provide environmental protection interests with substantial power to influence the agency. As described by Hoberg (1997), environmental litigants have used the courts to uphold these laws, blocking timber sales and restricting cutting methods on national forests. Hoberg contrasts federal forest management before and after the 1970s, with the earlier period marked by greater agency discretion and less overt environmental protection. Results from the four forest pairs indicate that state forest policy in the 1990s resembles federal forest policy prior to 1970: State forest officials face relatively few legal restrictions on timber production and almost no citizen power to appeal decisions.

Third, forest planning documents direct federal officials more than state officials to undertake activities that favor environmental protection. Recall from chapter 6 that forest plans for national forests tend to require greater environmental protection than do state forest plans—via timber stand improvement, "leave trees," riparian protection, regeneration harvest openings, and land use zones. Thus, agency members following plan guidelines pursue environmental protection efforts more at the federal level than at the state level.

Taken together, such differences in rules and the power of citizens seeking influence explain why federal agency officials exhibit systematically greater efforts to provide environmental protection outputs than do state officials. The dominant role of rules created by elected officials supports the extension of the functional theory of federalism to explain agency policy in a federal system. Even though agency officials aren't subject to electoral pressure, they are subject to constraints from legislators and executives who are, and these elected officials can significantly affect agency policy performance through rules.

Citizen Participation in Policy Processes

The ability of citizens to participate in and influence public policy is the hallmark of a democratic system. One significant venue for such participation is agency policymaking. Thus, the third measure of policy performance in this analysis is citizen participation in agency policy processes.

Important state-federal differences are evident in participation patterns. Not only did federal officials undertake greater efforts to solicit public input for policymaking, but the citizen interests participating also varied; commodity interests were more active and influential at the state level, whereas preservation interests were more active and influential at the federal level. Explanations for these differences include legal mandates, planning laws, agency composition, forest uses promoted, the geographic location of citizenry, and job mobility.

A fundamental rule affecting citizen participation patterns is the agency's statutory mandate. Recall that the USDA Forest Service has a multiple-use mandate, with a variety of goals to be pursued and no single goal described as dominant. In contrast, state statutes include language suggesting timber, or revenue production more generally, as a dominant goal. Citizens are aware of these mandates, which affect their participation in agency policymaking. One citizen favoring preservation in Oregon explained, "On the national forests, the same group of people deals with forestry, fish, and water quality issues, whereas the state is more fragmented by resource, so it's more difficult to communicate on nontimber issues." Another said, "We have less communication with state officials because their mandate is more narrow—to make revenue for the trusts."

The narrower mandate on state forests can lead state officials to weigh the importance of particular constituencies differently than do federal officials. One member of an Oregon county government who favored timber described sharp differences in communication with state and federal officials:

> The state district forester attends our meetings periodically and informs us about state plans and harvest projections, and the state forester attends our annual meeting. With the trust relationship, state officials recognize our importance as a primary beneficiary. But to national officials, we're just one among many constituencies, no more important than any other.

Differences in legal mandates also are evident in laws relating to planning processes. As described in chapter 6, none of the state forest agencies faced legally prescribed forest planning processes. In contrast, federal agency officials were required by the NFMA and NEPA to provide formal mechanisms for soliciting public participation and input. Thus, there are important differences in the weights given to particular citizen interests in forest planning, which can discourage some citizens from participating. For example, one citizen in Washington who favored timber expressed frustration at communicating with federal officials: "I don't provide much input on national forest projects because it's frustrating to spend a day or two analyzing documents and sending in comments that I know will be dumped out of a mailbag and considered equally among many other comments." Another citizen who favored timber was discouraged by the many legal and administrative requirements established for national forest planning: "The national forest has too much red tape, too many hoops to jump through. If I bring them a good idea, they can't go with it. Hell, if they had a cockroach infestation at their offices, it would probably take a year to get through the red tape to get the exterminator in."

In fulfilling NFMA and NEPA planning process requirements, federal officials provide more public meetings and mailings to encourage public input than do state officials. Preservation interests are likely to use these avenues in communicating with agency officials, especially if they perceive that such communication can influence forest policy. For example, several citizens in Oregon who favored preservation cited the formal public comment processes as making their involvement more accessible on the national forest than on state forests. Likewise, preservation proponents in Indiana said that the federal agency's public notification efforts—including scoping letters, quarterly newsletters, and personal phone calls—were helpful for staying in touch.

In contrast, timber interests are less likely to communicate with federal officials through these methods because they often are discouraged by their perceived inability to influence policy. One citizen who favored timber commented,

> The national folks like to play the numbers game, saying, "We had X number of people at this planning meeting representing many different interests." But the input they get doesn't matter in setting policies—the real decisions are made in Washington [D.C.].

Clearly, timber interests make less use of these methods than do preservation interests.

Another legal constraint that favors the influence of preservation over timber interests in federal forest policymaking is the appeals process established under the NFMA and NEPA. The appeals process allows people who are opposed to timber harvesting and other vegetative manipulation activities on national forests to halt or delay such activities. In contrast, no laws or regulations can force federal officials to provide timber. Thus, for the national forest, the deck is stacked in favor of people who wish to block commodity provision. In fact, numerous appeals in the past few years by environmental advocacy groups have led to delays in federal forest officials putting planned sales up for bid. On state forests, however, the opposite is true: Few laws or regulations provide for preservation interests to pursue effectively administrative appeals of decisions to provide timber, so the deck is stacked in favor of those who favor commodity provision.

In addition to legal constraints, agency composition plays an important role in patterns of communication and perceived influence. Preservation-oriented citizens report feeling more comfortable and influential in communicating with officials specializing in nontimber aspects of forest management, such as botany and wildlife biology. These specialists can provide greater attention to watersheds, soil protection, species habitat, and other nontimber forest resources than can timber specialists and forester generalists who are responsible for a wide range of resources. As one citizen in Ohio who favored preservation said, "I talk to federal officials more because with their specialists they are receptive to a broader spectrum of interests." Similarly, another person favoring preservation indicated that she felt more comfortable contacting the federal agency than the state agency because the former is staffed with a botanist who understands her concerns.

Conversely, state agencies include more personnel specializing in timber, which engenders closer ties to citizens favoring commodity uses. For example, one citizen in Washington who worked in the timber industry commented, "I have a better rapport with state personnel because I know nearly everyone in the regional office. Federal personnel include more of a cross-section of different personnel, with timber just a small part of the staff, so I don't know as many of them."

Thus, differences in the range of agency positions foster different patterns of communication and perceived influence.

Another important factor accounting for differences in participation and influence across levels of governance is forest uses promoted. Most timber interests report that their greatest levels of communication with agency officials occur during the course of timber sales, and (as described in chapter 3) state officials sell a significantly higher volume of timber than do federal officials. Through bidding, contract discussions, and harvesting activities, timber purchasers and loggers interact with agency officials to conduct timber operations. This situation creates a feedback loop: Timber interests communicate more with state officials, which reinforces higher state timber provision, which in turn reinforces more communication with timber interests.

Protimber citizens also develop close ties with state agency officials through other forest activities and programs. There is an especially close relationship between state agency officials and timber interests in Indiana, with cooperation in forestry programs, such as Project Learning Tree (an educational program aimed at school children), logger training, cost-sharing arrangements, and management of private timberlands. Timber professionals may contract to perform TSI work on state forests. These citizens work on a professional level with state forestry officials, as contractors and knowledgeable practitioners giving and receiving advice about forest management techniques. Such close working relationships between timber interests and state officials stand in sharp contrast to timber interests' interactions with federal officials, who provide fewer timber sale opportunities and do not generally contract for TSI work.

Another factor affecting citizen communication and influence involves the geographic location of stakeholders. By definition, national forests belong to all U.S. citizens, whereas state forests are owned by state residents. Citizens outside a given state have legal standing to influence policy on a national forest—to which they can claim ownership—in that state more readily than to influence policy on a state forest, to which they cannot claim ownership. Most national forest stakeholders live hundreds or thousands of miles from a given national forest, whereas state forest stakeholders live in closer proximity. Differences in geographic location are associated with different forest policy goals; studies have shown that people living closer to a natural resource tend to favor its use for economic development, and those living farther away are more likely to support preservation (Nash 1982; Tremblay and Dunlap 1978; Lowe and Pinhey 1982). Therefore it is not surprising that environmental interests are more active and influential on national forests. As one citizen said, "Environmental groups have a bigger impact at the national level because for thirty-two cents [the price of a postage stamp] anyone in any state can hold up a timber sale on any national forest."

Finally, an important factor affecting patterns of communication and perceived influence is job mobility. As described in chapter 8, state officials tend to remain in one location longer than do federal officials. Thus, they are more likely to forge long-term relationships with forest neighbors, who are more likely to favor commodity use than are those living farther away. As one timber proponent indicated, "National officials tend to move in and out a lot, so we don't know them as well as the state officials."

In sum, state-federal differences in citizen participation are caused by several factors. First, federal officials face stricter legal requirements, such as statutory mandates and planning laws, that give standing to a broad array of citizen interests. This situation encourages preservation interests to participate more in federal forest policy, whereas commodity interests participate more in state forest policy. Second, the wider variety of natural resource specialists employed in federal agency offices encourages citizens who favor nontimber goals to communicate with federal officials more than with state policymakers. Third, the higher quantity of timber produced on state forests increases state officials' communications with timber interests. Moreover, in some states timber interests are closely tied to forest agency officials through contract work and development of forestry programs. Fourth, the geographic location of citizenry gives federal officials a large number of constituents located far away from the forest, whereas state forest constituents are limited by state borders. To the extent that citizens who are farther from a natural resource tend to favor preservation and those who are closer tend to favor economic use, this situation tilts citizen interests for national forests toward preservation and citizen interests for state forests toward timber. Finally, differences in

Figure 9.1. Web of Factors that Explain Differences in State-Federal Policy Performance

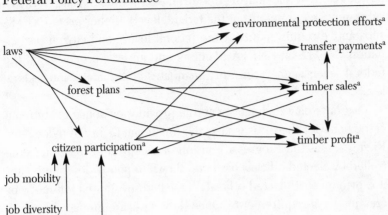

environmental protection efforts[a]

transfer payments[a]

laws

forest plans

timber sales[a]

citizen participation[a]

timber profit[a]

job mobility

job diversity

scope of jurisdiction

[a]Policy performance variables include environmental protection efforts, transfer payments, timber sales, timber profit, and citizen participation.

job mobility make it easier for state forest officials to build ties to local communities, where predominant goals are more likely to emphasize economic development of forest resources.

Conceptual Model to Explain State-Federal Differences in Forest Policy

Understanding the factors affecting bureaucratic behavior, as discussed in chapters 6 through 8, allows explanation of the state-federal policy performance differences discussed in chapters 3 through 5. Of course, relationships among these items are not straightforward or simple. As illustrated in Figure 9.1, the analysis in this chapter suggests myriad direct and indirect effects of laws, forest plans, and citizen participation.

Laws

Laws play a central role in affecting policy performance. As shown in Figure 9.1, laws have a direct impact on environmental protection

(NFMA substantive requirements at the federal level), transfer payments (revenue-sharing requirements), timber sales (NFMA substantive requirements at the federal level), timber profit (NFMA substantive requirements at the federal level), and citizen participation (NFMA and NEPA planning and appeals processes, at the federal level; agency statutory mandates at the state and federal levels).

That laws play such a critical role provides evidence for bureaucratic behavior theory as well as the functional theory of federalism. First, even as the Progressive vision of a neutral bureaucracy controlled by elected officials has been shown to poorly describe reality, it is evident that elected officials can wield substantial influence by creating legal requirements. Once these laws are in place, they can continue to affect agency behavior for many years into the future. The substantial impact that laws have on federal-level public forest policy are in line with Hoberg's (1997) description of the USDA Forest Service after 1970.

Second, it is apparent that the functional theory of federalism can be extended to explain agency policymaking in a federal system. Although agency officials are not elected, they nevertheless are powerfully influenced by laws created by elected officials. Given the ascending role of the bureaucracy in the United States over time, extending the functional theory of federalism to agency policymaking is significant. Clearly, it does matter at what level policy authority is vested in a federal system because different levels are likely to yield different policy performance.

Forest Plans

Forest plans, which are created by agency officials but also may be subject to influence from citizens and laws created by elected officials, directly affect environmental protection, timber sales, and timber profit. At the federal level, planning laws and citizen participation lead to forest plans that constrain agency officials' pursuit of timber provision. In contrast, state forest officials do not face statutory requirements about what to include in forest plans or who should have input into these plans. As a result, forest plans at the state level are less likely to constrain officials' pursuit of timber. Differences in forest plan guidelines contribute to greater timber provision and profitability at the state level but greater environmental protection efforts at the federal level.

Citizen Participation

Citizen participation, which is directly affected by laws, job diversity within the agency, forest uses promoted, scope of jurisdiction (geographic location of citizenry), and job mobility, accounts for several state-federal differences in policy performance. First, citizens have been considerably more successful in forcing agency officials to reduce timber harvest levels on national forests than on state forests. Legal requirements to involve citizens in national forest planning and to allow citizen appeals of policy choices have given a potent weapon to citizens who wish to block commodity provision on national forests. Conversely, on state forests, citizens have little ability to stop timber sales.

Second, beyond timber harvest levels, citizens have exerted influence on harvest techniques used on national forests, which affect timber profitability. Federal officials have described choices about harvest techniques more on the basis of avoiding citizen complaints (and appeals) than on maximizing economic returns. At the same time, the threat of citizen legal action has deterred some potential timber purchasers from bidding for timber sales on national forests. In contrast, state forests have not been much affected by preservation interests; timber interests are more active and influential at this level.

Third, citizen pressure accounts for differences in agency environmental protection efforts. Preservation interests have influenced federal officials more than state officials to undertake environmental protection efforts. Citizens living thousands of miles away from a particular forest, who are likely to favor preservation over economic uses, have greater opportunities to influence policymaking on that forest if it is a national forest rather than a state forest. Although residents living near a national forest may feel a sense of ownership, that forest is legally owned by all citizens of the United States.

Other Factors

It is important to recognize that Figure 9.1 indicates factors explaining state-federal differences in forest policy performance, rather than factors affecting forest policy performance more generally. This distinction is important because some factors that are likely to affect policy performance did not account for differences in this analysis. For example, the beliefs of agency officials have been shown to affect policy choices significantly across a variety of sectors. In the four forest pairs I examined, the beliefs of agency officials were fundamentally similar across levels of governance, so although this factor may be important in policymaking, it cannot explain differences in policy performance.

Other factors from bureaucratic behavior theory that may affect agency policymaking but did not exhibit systematic state-federal differences in this study include homogeneity of beliefs in the agency community and budget incentives. The degree to which such factors exhibit systematic state-federal differences in other policy sectors is an open question that could affect the degree to which state and federal policy performance differs.

Conclusion

Explaining differences in policy performance is not straightforward. Insights from the functional theory of federalism and bureaucratic behavior theory provide pieces to the puzzle. On the basis of my analysis, I argue that systematic federal-state differences do exist and that they can be explained by the interplay of many factors. Fundamentally, the most important factors are rules and citizen pressure, which lead state agencies to excel in timber provision, profitability, and revenue sharing, whereas federal agencies lead in environmental protection and citizen participation in policy processes.

10 Implications for Policy in a Federal System

As described in the opening pages of this book, citizens and policy-makers alike continue to debate the merits of devolving policy authority from federal to state levels. Questions about forest and other natural resource policies in a federal system are salient and important to many people. Disagreements about the appropriate use and management of these resources have resulted in lawsuits, petitions, legal reforms, legislative proposals, illegal actions, and physical violence.

In arguing about appropriate levels of governance, proponents of state primacy claim that states provide more effective and efficient policy administration, whereas proponents of federal control claim that federal officials are better able to pursue multiple policy goals. Unfortunately, such normative claims rarely are accompanied by empirical evidence about differences across levels of governance.

The results presented in this book provide such evidence. Through careful case selection and analysis of one policy sector—public forest management—in which state and federal levels of governance exercise authority, this analysis addresses two fundamental questions: Do state and federal agency public forest policy performances differ systematically? If so, why are there such differences?

The results illuminate not only forest and natural resource policy but also other areas where public policy involves tradeoffs and decisions within a system of multiple jurisdictions. These findings have implications for natural resource management, public agencies, and federalism.

Summary of Findings

In the preceding chapters I examined state-federal differences in public forest agency policy performance and factors affecting policymaking. Through systematic comparisons of a variety of factors in four carefully selected forest pairs, I discovered several important patterns.

The analysis in chapter 3 reveals systematic differences in timber provision and fiscal results. Across the forest pairs, state forests provided much higher timber sales than did national forests, in terms of gross board-feet and in terms of portion of annual tree growth. The greater emphasis on timber at the state level is reflected in the substantially higher percentage of agency operating budgets devoted to timber provision, compared to federal agency budgets.

In comparing fiscal performance, one important measure is net profit from timber provision. Where government activities are not cost-effective, economic losses accrue to the taxpayers funding them. State timber provision exhibits lower unit costs and higher unit revenues, for a higher unit net profit than federal timber provision.

Another important measure of fiscal performance is the transfer of funds to local governments. This output is particularly important in a federal system in which resource ownership by one level of government impinges on the capacity of another level to collect revenue. In the case of public forests, land that is owned by a federal or state agency is not available for generation of property tax revenue. Instead, counties receive a share of revenue generated on the forest. Thus, local government officials have a strong interest in alternative revenue possibilities from the forest land. My analysis indicates that state agencies transfer substantially greater revenue sums to county governments than do federal agencies.

Chapter 4 compares federal to state environmental protection efforts. Although this performance measure is critically important in natural resource policy, it also is representative of one side of a trade-off that is common across a variety of policy sectors: economic development versus noneconomic goals. Here, a composite indicator of environmental protection efforts includes ecosystem-level management, rare species identification and protection, ecosystem research and monitoring, and soil and watershed protection and improvement. Across the four forest pairs, federal officials undertook greater environmental protection efforts.

Chapter 5 investigates the third policy performance measure: citizen participation in agency policymaking. The rise of the "administrative state" in the United States has been accompanied by considerable debates over the role of citizens in agency policymaking; citizen participation has become, for some people, an end in itself. This study examines the degree to which agency officials encourage citizen participation and the patterns of citizen interests represented at different government levels. The findings reveal that, compared to state forest officials, federal officials devote more effort to encouraging public participation, and they receive a higher proportion of input from citizens favoring preservation. State officials, in contrast, receive a higher proportion of public input from those favoring timber.

Chapters 6 through 8 examine factors affecting agency policymaking, in search of state-federal differences to explain policy performance differences. Bureaucratic behavior theory suggests four types of influential variables: rules, citizens, agency officials' beliefs, and agency community.

For the rules variable, the laws and forest plan rules analyzed in chapter 6 exhibit distinct state-federal differences. On national forests, statutes such as the Multiple-Use, Sustained-Yield Act; the National Forest Management Act; and the National Environmental Policy Act, along with their implementing regulations, address decision-making processes and specific forest management techniques and purposes. These rules constrain federal officials' ability to increase timber provision, requiring numerous efforts to protect other resources, such as rare species. They also encourage public access and influence in policymaking. In addition, planning documents require federal officials to undertake substantial efforts to protect the forest environment and to involve the public in agency decision making.

State officials, in contrast, face fewer constraints on their ability to pursue activities such as timber sales that yield substantial, direct economic benefits. State forest agency mandates emphasize timber as a source of profit or revenue rather than as just one of many equally valued resources. State planning documents provide officials with greater freedom to pursue economic development without significant public input.

Budget rules explored in chapter 7 do not systematically differ between state and federal levels. Despite the oft-cited view that budget incentives such as the Knutsen-Vandenberg Act strongly encourage timber provision on national forests, evidence from the four forest pairs does not support budgets as a powerful determinant of which management activities agency officials undertake. Instead, most officials feel that they are unable to affect their budget levels significantly, no matter what strategies they pursue. Where officials do mention particular agency activities that they perceive will influence budgets, such activities do not differ significantly by level of government.

As discussed in chapter 8, three additional factors that are expected to influence agency policymaking are citizen pressure, agency officials' beliefs, and agency community. State-federal differences are evident in citizen influence but not in agency officials' beliefs or homogeneity of beliefs within an agency. First, citizens favoring preservation perceive greater influence among federal officials, whereas those favoring timber perceive greater influence among state officials. (This difference in perceived influence is similar to the differences in communications described in chapter 5.)

Second, officials' beliefs do not systematically differ by level of government. In particular, only two of fourteen questionnaire items reveal statistically significant beliefs about appropriate forest management.

Third, two attributes of agency community—employee turnover/relocation and variety of job positions—systematically differ by level of government. Compared to state forest agency officials, members of the federal agency community have significantly longer job tenures and higher geographic mobility within the agency—a combination that tends to breed a culture of conformity. The federal agency community includes a much wider variety of job positions, however, which makes it more difficult for members of an organization to share similar beliefs. The combination of these two attributes yields a similar level of homogeneity of members' beliefs between the state level and the federal level.

Chapter 9 employs the findings from factors affecting bureaucratic behavior to explain state-federal policy performance differences. First, lower timber sales volumes on the national forests stem largely from legal requirements, particularly in NFMA and NEPA, which require substantial preharvest work and provide citizens with power to block timber sales. Similarly, legal requirements cause higher unit costs for timber sale preparation on national forests; lower unit revenues are caused by an agency statutory mandate that encourages timber provision to be used as a tool rather than an end in itself, along with citizen opposition and legal limits on regeneration harvesting. This combination yields dramatically lower timber sale profits on the national forests than on the state forests. As a result of lower timber sales, federal officials transfer far less money to local governments than do state officials.

Second, greater environmental protection efforts on national forests are attributable primarily to rules. Whereas state agency legal mandates establish timber and revenue generation as dominant goals, the federal agency legal mandate emphasizes multiple uses without specifying a dominant goal. In addition, the NFMA places specific requirements on federal officials to protect species diversity, whereas no such law constrains state officials. Finally, rules in the forest planning documents, which guide management practices, emphasize environmental protection more at the federal level.

Third, citizen participation differences are caused by several related factors, which lead federal officials to undertake greater efforts to encourage citizen participation input and also lead to different patterns of communication across interest types: Preservation interests are more active at the federal level, whereas commodity interests are more active at the state level. Critical factors include agency statutory mandates, planning laws, agency composition, forest uses promoted, the geographic location of citizenry, and job mobility.

It is important to note that data analyses reveal several differences among states, as well as among the four national forest offices. For example, timber provision levels are substantially greater on Oregon state forests and Washington state forests than on Indiana state forests and Ohio state forests; likewise, timber provision is greater on Gifford Pinchot National Forest and Siuslaw National Forest than on Wayne

National Forest and Hoosier National Forest. I have not analyzed these differences here because the aim of this research is to understand how state and federal agency policy differs. The fact that systematic state-federal differences exist despite substantial variability between regions of the country strengthens the argument that the level of government does, indeed, affect agency policy.

It also is important to note that this study intentionally focuses on one time period, to compare state forest agency policy to federal forest agency policy at the same time. Thus, it does not speak to change over time, which obviously has occurred in forest policy. For example, it is possible that in an earlier era—such as prior to passage of NEPA in 1970 and NFMA in 1976—federal agency policymaking might have resembled state agency policymaking very closely. Instead, by examining differences at a single, more recent time point, this study aims to inform theoretical and policy issues of federalism and natural resource management.

Policy Implications for Natural Resource Management and Public Agencies

Public agencies play a critical role in natural resource policy. Forests, rangelands, wilderness areas, wildlife refuges, parks, and many other important natural resources remain in public control. This analysis provides results that are relevant to natural resource policies and public agencies. In particular, the findings are instructive for several important issues, including appropriate levels of governance, management of agency culture, and budgetary incentives.

Appropriate Levels of Governance for Natural Resource Management

The level of government that is most appropriate for natural resource policy depends on which performance criteria are valued. People who favor economic development and profitable resource use would be better served with state-level authority, whereas those favoring environmental protection and citizen participation, especially from noneconomic interests, would prefer federal-level control.

Current institutional arrangements reduce federal officials' ability to turn a profit on timber provision from national forests, which is an important fiscal outcome. Clearly, spending more money than is earned from timber sales does not provide net economic benefits to U.S. taxpayers. Money that is spent to sell timber on national forests benefits timber companies and their employees; it is doubtful whether most Americans would favor such a use of tax money in light of the financial losses. Those who justify the higher unit costs and lower unit revenues for federal timber on the basis of greater environmental protection must recognize that the goal of environmental protection would be served better by spending funds currently lost on timber sales to undertake efforts to protect the forest ecosystem. For example, had the $3,158,800 spent on timber sales in Siuslaw National Forest in fiscal year 1995 (which generated a $276,010 net loss) been spent on erosion control instead, the federal land would have more uncut forest as well as higher levels of water quality.

It is evident from this study that state control promises higher economic returns than does federal control. State foresters have greater freedom from constraints that hinder the provision of economic benefits and allow timber harvesting opponents to delay or block proposed sales. Thus, natural resources are more intensively managed for economic development at the state level. Conversely, federal foresters are more successful in pursuing policies without significant, direct economic benefits. One would be likely to find more management for environmental protection on national lands. Thus, neither federal nor state-level responsibility should be considered uniformly "better." Instead, the desirability of control by different levels of governance depends on the criteria used. The existence of responsibilities at both levels in a federal system provides opportunities for a mix of economic and environmental benefits.

The existence of multiple jurisdictions also provides the possibility of specialization across levels of governance, with each focusing on what it does best. Why shouldn't national forests be managed to generate nontimber benefits and state forests to generate economic benefits? Certainly, evidence suggests poor financial performance on national forests, and many environmental advocacy groups have called for cessation of all timber sales on national forests. A drawback of this specialization approach, however, is that managing exclusively for timber provision on state forests may reduce important environmental benefits. For example, state forests may provide critical habitat for certain species, without which the species could become extinct even as federal officials work to protect them on national forests.

Moreover, concentrating on economic benefits from state forests raises the question: Why should state governments continue to own forests, rather than selling them to private owners who might better manage forests for economic returns? If the reason is a responsibility to create income for trust beneficiaries, perhaps the states would do better by selling timber land and converting the assets into higher yielding investments. This question is not merely an academic musing. It involves real policy choices in natural resource management. For example, several scholars at the University of Washington, which receives trust revenue from state forest management, argue that the state should convert assets from forests to more lucrative investments, such as stocks (see Brune 1996).

Besides policy performance differences in outputs, one natural resource policy performance criterion centers on process. Forest agency officials undertake greater efforts to foster meaningful participation among a variety of citizens at the federal level. Such efforts do not mean that federal officials communicate equally with all citizen interest types; greater communication and influence come from those favoring preservation. State officials, in contrast, are more likely to communicate with, and be influenced by, citizens favoring timber. This difference does not support the arguments of people who advocate devolution as a means to give citizens greater input into policymaking. Although devolution is likely to give a greater proportional voice to a particular type of citizen interest, such as commodity proponents, devolving authority without changing underlying factors affecting officials' behavior is not likely to enhance widespread public involvement.

Management of Agency Culture

Administration of natural resource policy in the United States lies largely in the hands of public agencies. Officials in these agencies create and implement natural resource policies in central office head-quarters as well as in many dispersed field offices. An important question in natural resource policy is how an agency manages its organizational culture to coordinate employee behavior across numerous geographic locations. Kaufman's (1960) seminal work in USDA Forest Service administrative behavior suggests the importance of homogeneity of preferences and unity of mission. He argues that higher-level agency officials foster homogeneity and unity within the organization, in part through promotion from within and frequent employee relocation to tie individuals more closely to the agency than to citizens in a particular geographic location. "Esprit de corps" and shared common vision among agency officials are important reasons for USDA Forest Service policy successes (Clarke and McCool 1985).

Divergence from shared norms and preferences is likely to result, however, when the types of job positions within an organization become more diverse. When an organization hires more specialists with duties that are different from those in traditional job positions, a wider array of points of view is introduced into the organizational culture. Increasing job position diversity has occurred in the USDA Forest Service since it began to hire numerous resource specialists; interestingly, however, homogeneity of beliefs about forest resource use and management is no lower among federal officials than among state officials.

Two competing explanations for this similarity in homogeneity exist. Perhaps the similarity in disciplinary background (forestry) explains the similar levels of homogeneity. If so, an agency seeking homogeneity and unity should hire individuals with a common disciplinary background. In contrast, perhaps the Forest Service practices of emphasizing promotion from within—which increases average length of tenure—and fostering higher employee geographic mobility lead to similar levels of homogeneity. If this is true, an agency seeking homogeneity and unity should emphasize promotion from within and increasing officials' geographic mobility. Further analysis of factors contributing to intra-agency homogeneity is needed to determine which of these two variables is more important in managing agency culture to increase homogeneity of officials' preferences.

Budgetary Incentives

Many studies of public agencies and bureaucratic behavior emphasize the importance of budgetary resources. Evidence from my analysis supports the important role of budgets in affecting agency policies. Officials across the agencies consistently described budgetary resources as a key factor affecting their policymaking. Not only are budgets similarly important across levels of governance; budgetary incentives are similar as well. Neither state nor federal officials described strong incentives to provide certain outputs as a means to augment budgetary resources. In most forest pairs, external forces affecting budgetary resources available to agency officials leave little room for officials' strategic behavior to augment budgets. Institutional arrangements such as legislative budget allocation and authorization procedures reduce incentives for agency officials to emphasize certain forest outputs over others. Thus, the checks and balances inherent in the U.S. democratic governance system impede officials' ability to pursue budget maximization successfully.

An important result from this study addresses the common criticism that USDA Forest Service officials face substantial budgetary incentives to harvest timber regardless of net profitability (Budiansky 1991; O'Toole 1988; Rice 1989). The Knutsen-Vandenberg Act allows federal officials to retain a portion of gross receipts at the local level, for use in projects related to the timber sale area. Thus, on the surface, this provision seems to provide a strong incentive to sell more timber. Yet federal officials do not view the K-V Act as an important factor in timber sale decisions, and they may qualify for only limited amounts of funding for projects within a small geographic area. Thus, claims of widespread, negative impacts of the K-V Act miss the mark. Instead, below-cost timber sales are attributable to factors such as legal constraints that limit harvest techniques and require specific tasks that must precede timber sales, along with citizen appeals that block or delay timber sales.

Broader Implications for Federalism

Although this book focuses on one policy sector—public forests—the analysis has broader implications for public policy in federal systems.

My findings provide insight into several subjects, including the importance of rules, possibilities for innovation, interjurisdictional competition, citizen participation at different levels of governance, intergovernmental fiscal relations, and, perhaps most important theoretically, extension of the functional theory of federalism from elected to agency officials.

Importance of Rules

Rules matter in shaping policy performance; there are key differences between federal and state institutional arrangements that influence agency officials' behavior. Federal officials face greater institutional constraints affecting their activities than do state officials. These constraints contribute to lower levels of timber provision, at higher unit costs and lower unit revenues. Subsequently, less revenue is transferred to local governments.

At the same time, federal officials devote greater efforts toward environmental protection than do state officials. Moreover, federal laws encourage federal agency officials to solicit meaningful citizen participation in agency policymaking more than do state agency officials.

Thus, changes in institutional arrangements can provide a means to influence policy performance. Rules can be changed through elected representatives, who enact laws affecting agency official behavior. My analysis does not support the traditional view that state officials have different skills and beliefs than federal officials (White 1953). Instead, it supports more recent arguments in state resurgence literature, which suggest that state and federal agencies attract individuals whose characteristics and qualifications are similar (see Cigler 1993; Eisinger 1988). Thus, rather than depending on changing the characteristics of individual agency members, altering institutional arrangements is a viable strategy for changing agency policymaking.

Policy Innovations

An important potential benefit of federal systems is innovation. The existence of a variety of agencies and multiple jurisdictions provides opportunities for experimentation, adaptation, and adoption of successful policies. I find that state and federal agencies can provide innovation, but we should expect systematic differences in the types of innovation. Specifically, state agency innovations are more likely to focus on commodity provision and revenue enhancement, and federal agency innovations are expected to focus on innovations in noneconomic benefits such as environmental protection.

For example, an important innovation by Oregon state officials has been the creation of a Habitat Conservation Plan (HCP). An HCP is an agreement between the U.S. Fish and Wildlife Service (or the National Marine Fisheries Service) and a nonfederal party, such as a state, to allow an incidental "take" of an endangered species in exchange for planned activities to promote that species' success (Nelson 1999). Landowners propose to conduct specific activities while complying with Endangered Species Act requirements. By proposing to provide late-successional habitat in different locations throughout time ("structure-based management"), Oregon state officials can avoid having substantial acreage where commercial timber harvest is prohibited. Similarly, Washington state forest officials have developed an HCP to allow continued high levels of harvesting. In addition, Washington state officials have been proactive in leasing communication tower sites on public forest land, to generate income.

Federal agency officials, on the other hand, are innovating in policies whose main goal is not to increase timber provision. In Washington and Oregon, national forests include innovative adaptive management areas that are designed, in part, as purposive experiments to learn about effects of various practices on forest ecosystem conditions (see, for example, Shindler, Steel, and List 1996). Thus, innovation type varies across levels of governance, with lower levels more likely to innovate in revenue-enhancing and economic development activities and higher levels more likely to innovate in outputs such as environmental protection. In other policy areas, innovations might differ by level of governance according to their contributions to economic development.

Interjurisdictional Competition

In a federal system, an important benefit is the existence of multiple jurisdictions, which gives citizens opportunities to compare performance and seek change in jurisdictions that don't perform as well. Federalism scholars often point to such responsiveness as a critical benefit of federal systems of governance, often focusing on theoretical arguments about how the existence of multiple jurisdictions enhances responsiveness (see, for example, Ostrom 1987).

This phenomenon is evident in public forest policy. For example, it is clear that federal officials face more constraints that require public access to forest planning and decision making. Citizens who are knowledgeable about federal forest policy processes have sought to increase access to state processes. In Ohio, preservation interests pursued, through legislators, constraints that required agency officials to conduct more formal, open decision-making processes. In Oregon, environmental advocates sued the state forest agency, claiming that its decision-making processes were arbitrary and demanding greater access and more open processes. These attempts to move state agency policymaking in the direction of federal agency policymaking affected officials' behavior. Ohio state forest officials enacted a moratorium on commercial harvesting from a particular forest and undertook greater efforts to inform the public about planned forest activities. Oregon state forest officials created rules codifying existing planning processes.

Citizen Participation

Citizens can press for agencies to fulfill particular goals through a variety of channels. In a democratic system of government, the degree to which citizens are allowed to participate in agency decision-making processes is an important issue. This question emphasizes the fundamental tension between agency officials' expertise and responsiveness because relying on bureaucratic expertise that is insulated from public opinion is likely to decrease bureaucratic responsiveness to particular citizens' demands. This tension is evident in forest management: Public forest professionals rely on their judgment about how to best manage forest resources but also may be required to solicit citizen participation in decision making.

Advocates of devolution argue that lower levels of governance encourage greater citizen participation and influence. In smaller government jurisdictions, they argue, the voice of one citizen is proportionally greater than it is in larger jurisdictions. Moreover, for most citizens, state government seats are situated closer than is Washington, D.C. This view fits Thomas Jefferson's vision of a democratic nation with governmental authority vested primarily in lower-level jurisdictions.

This intuitive notion does not hold up under empirical investigation, however. The analysis presented in this book suggests that, in fact, federal-level officials tend to promote greater citizen participation. Across the four forest pairs, federal officials undertook greater efforts to encourage meaningful citizen participation in policymaking.

Another state-federal difference in participation is the degree to which citizens with different interests are active and influential. As several scholars have suggested, citizens whose primary goal is not economic benefits are more active at higher levels of governance (Peterson 1981; Heclo 1978; Sabatier 1974; Walker 1983). Across the four forest pairs, federal agency officials communicate more with parties favoring noneconomic benefits (preservation), and state officials communicate more with parties seeking economic benefits (timber). Consequently, those favoring preservation perceive greater influence with federal officials, whereas those favoring timber perceive greater influence with state officials.

For people who value public input and influence, higher levels of governance may be more appropriate. Of course, greater public involvement often reduces the ability of bureaucratic experts to carry out activities in a timely and cost-effective manner. This tradeoff should be an important consideration in decisions about the appropriate level of governmental responsibility.

Intergovernmental Fiscal Relations

Although this analysis emphasizes comparisons of state and federal levels of governance, it is important to note that federalism is more than competition among jurisdictions. An important literature in intergovernmental relations focuses on interactions among officials at various levels of governance. A key component of intergovernmental relations is fiscal relations—the flow of funding and influence across levels of governance (Swartz and Peck 1990; Oates 1991).

Intergovernmental revenue sharing is especially important for natural resources that are publicly owned. Lower levels of governance, such as counties, that rely heavily on property taxes are greatly affected by public ownership of natural resources because public land owners generally do not pay property taxes. In fact, in regions where federal officials attempt to purchase land for public ownership, there often is opposition from parties who are concerned about maintaining the property tax base for local government jurisdictions such as counties and school districts.

To make up for this property tax shortfall, public owners may be required to share a portion of revenues with local governments. Each of the eight public forests in this study is subject to revenue-sharing requirements. Systematic differences are evident in revenue-sharing amounts: State agencies share more funds with local governments than do federal agencies. From the local government's perspective, then, the question of which level of government owns and manages public forests is critical. In fact, local government officials often are at the forefront of proposals to transfer federally managed lands into state or local ownership (Larson 1995; *Register-Guard* 1996).

Extending Functional Theory of Federalism to Bureaucrats

Finally, and perhaps most important theoretically, this analysis extends the functional theory of federalism to nonelected bureaucrats. According to this theory, elected officials face electoral pressures that affect the policies they pursue. Those at lower levels of governance emphasize developmental policies, which enhance the jurisdictions' resources by increasing business and employee tax revenues. Because mobility of firms and individuals across lower levels of jurisdiction often is high, local officials who emphasize policies that hurt economic development spur firms to leave, which results in voter displeasure and elected officials being voted out of office. Thus, elected officials at lower levels of governance who champion policies that promote economic development are more likely to win and remain in office. In contrast, elected officials at higher levels of governance do not face firms with such high mobility; thus, they can pursue policies that are less favorable to economic development without a high likelihood that they will be defeated in the next election.

Given the growing role of civil servants in shaping and carrying out public policy, we should learn about whether and how the functional theory of federalism applies to their actions. I argue that although agency officials are not elected, they are greatly affected by rules created by elected officials. These rules foster bureaucratic behavior to promote economic development more at lower levels of governance and environmental protection at higher levels of governance.

Such differences in rules are not limited to the forest policy sector. For example, environmental and other regulatory policies involve tradeoffs between economic development and goals such as clean air and citizen health. Similarly, debates in health care policy center on cost savings versus full coverage, and those in welfare policy often focus on cost savings versus assistance to all needy individuals. Moreover, it is important to note that rules from NEPA and the Administrative Procedure Act apply to more than just public forest management; all federal agencies are bound by these requirements. Further study outside of forest policy would provide additional empirical evidence about the quantity and types of constraints facing bureaucrats at different levels of governance.

Conclusion

The question of appropriate jurisdictions for various government activities continues to be a fundamental issue in American politics. Answers to this question should be based on solid empirical evidence about policy performance across levels of governance. Ironically, despite the vigor with which advocates for greater federal or state control pursue their arguments, little research has compared policy performance systematically across levels of governance. Instead, federalism scholarship has emphasized understanding difficulties in implementing federal policy directives at state and local levels (see Pressman and Wildavsky 1984; Derthick 1971). Other studies have examined policy at just one level of governance (Lowry 1992; Rabe 1986; Ringquist 1990; Clarke and McCool 1985). Thus, in this book I provide empirical evidence about policymaking in different jurisdictions within a federal system.

As the results show, it does make a difference whether policy responsibility lies in a higher or lower level of governance. Federal agency officials who are creating and implementing public policy face systematically different policy process constraints than do state agency officials. These differences affect officials' behavior and policy performance.

Advocates of policy change may pursue two divergent strategies. First, they may advocate transferring policy authority to the level of governance that is most likely to perform as they prefer. Citizens who favor policy outputs without substantial, direct economic benefits, for example, would do well to advocate authority at higher levels of governance. Second, they may advocate changes in rules. Alterations in agency officials' behavior may be achieved by changing the laws that influence their policy choices.

The likelihood of success under these different strategies cannot be determined from this analysis. Further attention to this question would provide valuable insights. In addition, rigorous, systematic state-federal comparisons in other policy sectors could prove useful in understanding federalism more broadly. It is time to move beyond normative debates about federalism and focus greater attention on careful empirical comparisons of specified policy sectors across levels of governance. Only through such work will we be prepared to make informed decisions about appropriate responsibilities in federal systems.

Appendix A
Methods

For this project I relied on a variety of methods, including interviews, observation, and document analysis. Using a triangulation of techniques and data sources, I sought to enhance the reliability of my findings.

Interviews

A large portion of the data come from semi-structured interviews, which are useful for obtaining large amounts of data, tapping into information from a wide variety of individuals, and discovering complex interconnections in social relationships (Marshall and Rossman 1989: 102). Interview data are subject to distortion, however, from miscommunication or even untruthful interviewees. Furthermore, such information is based on individual perceptions rather than on actual behavior. To overcome these limitations, I conducted interviews with several people regarding the same events or phenomena, to check for consistency of explanations. In addition, I used other data-gathering methods to supplement interviews.

Interview data come from a wide range of individuals who are most closely involved in making decisions about how the forests are managed. These individuals include agency officials in line and staff positions, from field workers to state forestry department chiefs and national forest supervisors. Although not all of these individuals supervise employees and allocate budgets, each has responsibilities for making management decisions and providing input into forest decision making. The interviewees included in this research constitute a cross-section of similar areas of responsibility within each agency, including timber sales planning and administration, wildlife, recreation, environmental protection, legislative relations, public education and communication, budget management, and overall program/agency management. To facilitate open and honest communications, I assured all interviewees that no comments would be associated with particular individuals in any written reports. Thus, I have not attributed any quoted text to named individuals.

All of the interviewees were open and accommodating in their communications. Although a few interviews took place over the phone, most interviewees participated in multiple, in-person interview sessions, each lasting at least one hour. Repeated contacts and in-person visits provided me with opportunities to build trust and witness nonverbal cues.

The interviews were semi-structured. Interviewees responded to a set of specific questions, but I did not ask the questions in the same precise words or order. Instead, interviewees answered questions during the course of a continuing discussion, as I attempted to link one topic logically to another. This approach provided me with flexibility to follow up responses, seek clarification, and probe more deeply into interesting statements. Although I chose not to record conversations on tape, I took notes carefully, and, for several sessions, the interviewees checked them and endorsed their accuracy. In total, I conducted in-depth interviews with ninety-four officials, totaling more than 150 hours of conversation.

To gain further insights and perspectives, I conducted phone interviews with citizen participants who were involved in forest policy. I purposefully selected the interviewees on the basis that agency personnel listed them as "key contacts" or because other interviewees suggested them as important people to contact. I encouraged them to speak freely and honestly, with the assurance of confidentiality. Most citizen interviews lasted ten to fifteen minutes, with discussion focusing on communication levels, perceived influence, and perceived agency support for the individual's or group's particular goals. In total, sixty-eight citizen contacts participated in such interviews.

Observation

Systematic observation can provide useful insights beyond individual perceptions. My observations for this study focused on public meetings, including attendance at a series of "community of interest meetings" conducted by federal forest officials.

Document Analysis

A third type of data comes from documents. Analysis of written documents provides objective data classification, useful documentation of major events, and the opportunity to generalize (Marshall and Rossman 1989: 95, 102). Participants shared numerous documents, including reports, plans, budget proposals, accounting spreadsheets, internal memos, and maps.

One type of written document that I used in this research was a confidential three-part questionnaire administered to agency personnel (see below). In the first part, respondents indicated, on a five-point rating scale, their beliefs about specific management issues. They also indicated their perceptions about their agency's activities with regard to these issues. In the second part, respondents shared their perspectives on the amount of influence various factors have in determining agency activities. Finally, the third part of the questionnaire provided space for respondents to describe who they considered to be their key contacts, as well as the nature of their communication with these contacts. To encourage honest and accurate responses, I assured participants that no responses would be attributed to particular individuals. Overall, seventy-five of eighty-seven agency members returned questionnaires, for a response rate of 86 percent.

QUESTIONNAIRE

PART 1a: FOREST MANAGEMENT ISSUES

Please circle the response that best indicates how you feel about the following issues as they relate to land managed by your agency. Also indicate the degree to which you believe agency policies favor or disfavor these items:

(Example) Using prescribed fire as a management tool

I . . . Strongly favor Favor Neither favor nor disfavor Disfavor Strongly disfavor

Agency policies . . . Strongly favor Favor Neither favor nor disfavor Disfavor Strongly disfavor

1. Increasing, or establishing new, recreational user fees

I . . . Strongly favor Favor Neither favor nor disfavor Disfavor Strongly disfavor

Agency policies . . . Strongly favor Favor Neither favor nor disfavor Disfavor Strongly disfavor

2. Including clear cutting as a silvicultural option

I . . . Strongly favor Favor Neither favor nor disfavor Disfavor Strongly disfavor

Agency policies . . . Strongly favor Favor Neither favor nor disfavor Disfavor Strongly disfavor

3. Giving extra weight to local economic considerations in decision making

I . . . Strongly favor Favor Neither favor nor disfavor Disfavor Strongly disfavor

Agency policies . . . Strongly favor Favor Neither favor nor disfavor Disfavor Strongly disfavor

4. Actively converting non-native stands to native stands

I . . . Strongly favor Favor Neither favor nor disfavor Disfavor Strongly disfavor

Agency policies . . . Strongly favor Favor Neither favor nor disfavor Disfavor Strongly disfavor

5. Increasing efforts to seek public input in management decisions

I . . .   Strongly favor   Favor   Neither favor nor disfavor   Disfavor   Strongly disfavor

Agency policies . . . Strongly favor   Favor   Neither favor nor disfavor   Disfavor   Strongly disfavor

6. Managing for forest ecosystems, even if that means reducing direct benefits to people

I . . .   Strongly favor   Favor   Neither favor nor disfavor   Disfavor   Strongly disfavor

Agency policies . . . Strongly favor   Favor   Neither favor nor disfavor   Disfavor   Strongly disfavor

7. Increasing the following forest uses:

Timber

I . . .   Strongly favor   Favor   Neither favor nor disfavor   Disfavor   Strongly disfavor

Agency policies . . . Strongly favor   Favor   Neither favor nor disfavor   Disfavor   Strongly disfavor

Oil/gas/minerals

I . . .   Strongly favor   Favor   Neither favor nor disfavor   Disfavor   Strongly disfavor

Agency policies . . . Strongly favor   Favor   Neither favor nor disfavor   Disfavor   Strongly disfavor

Hunting/fishing

I . . .   Strongly favor   Favor   Neither favor nor disfavor   Disfavor   Strongly disfavor

Agency policies . . . Strongly favor   Favor   Neither favor nor disfavor   Disfavor   Strongly disfavor

Developed camping

I . . .   Strongly favor   Favor   Neither favor nor disfavor   Disfavor   Strongly disfavor

Agency policies . . . Strongly favor   Favor   Neither favor nor disfavor   Disfavor   Strongly disfavor

Hiking trails

I . . .   Strongly favor   Favor   Neither favor nor disfavor   Disfavor   Strongly disfavor

Agency policies . . . Strongly favor   Favor   Neither favor nor disfavor   Disfavor   Strongly disfavor

Horse trails

I . . .   Strongly favor   Favor   Neither favor nor disfavor   Disfavor   Strongly disfavor

Agency policies . . . Strongly favor   Favor   Neither favor nor disfavor   Disfavor   Strongly disfavor

Off road vehicle trails

I . . .   Strongly favor   Favor   Neither favor nor disfavor   Disfavor   Strongly disfavor

Agency policies . . . Strongly favor   Favor   Neither favor nor disfavor   Disfavor   Strongly disfavor

Wilderness/preservation areas

I . . .   Strongly favor   Favor   Neither favor nor disfavor   Disfavor   Strongly disfavor

Agency policies . . . Strongly favor   Favor   Neither favor nor disfavor   Disfavor   Strongly disfavor

Other: _____

I . . .   Strongly favor   Favor   Neither favor nor disfavor   Disfavor   Strongly disfavor

Agency policies . . . Strongly favor   Favor   Neither favor nor disfavor   Disfavor   Strongly disfavor

PART 1b: INFLUENCE ON FOREST MANAGEMENT ACTIVITIES

Please indicate, on a scale of 1 to 5, the amount of influence you believe that each of the following has on determining management activities on the forest(s) for which you have responsibility:

	Very influential		Somewhat influential		No influence
Existing laws and regulations:	5	4	3	2	1
Existing forest uses:	5	4	3	2	1
Forest Plan or Land Management Manual:	5	4	3	2	1
Expertise/beliefs of agency personnel on the forest(s):	5	4	3	2	1
Higher agency officials, through					
evaluating & communicating with subordinates:	5	4	3	2	1
budgets:	5	4	3	2	1
Legislature, through					
communicating with agency personnel:	5	4	3	2	1
budgets:	5	4	3	2	1
Local residents, through					
communicating with agency personnel:	5	4	3	2	1
administrative or court challenges:	5	4	3	2	1
pressure on legislators:	5	4	3	2	1
People living outside the local area, through					
communicating with agency personnel:	5	4	3	2	1
administrative or court challenges:	5	4	3	2	1
pressure on legislators:	5	4	3	2	1
People favoring timber, through					
communicating with agency personnel:	5	4	3	2	1
administrative or court challenges:	5	4	3	2	1
pressure on legislators:	5	4	3	2	1
People favoring oil/gas/mineral uses, through					
communicating with agency personnel:	5	4	3	2	1
administrative or court challenges:	5	4	3	2	1
pressure on legislators:	5	4	3	2	1
People favoring hunting/fishing, through					
communicating with agency personnel:	5	4	3	2	1
administrative or court challenges:	5	4	3	2	1
pressure on legislators:	5	4	3	2	1

	Very influential		Somewhat influential		No influence
People favoring developed camping, through					
communicating with agency personnel:	5	4	3	2	1
administrative or court challenges:	5	4	3	2	1
pressure on legislators:	5	4	3	2	1
People favoring hiking, through					
communicating with agency personnel:	5	4	3	2	1
administrative or court challenges:	5	4	3	2	1
pressure on legislators:	5	4	3	2	1
People favoring horse riding, through					
communicating with agency personnel:	5	4	3	2	1
administrative or court challenges:	5	4	3	2	1
pressure on legislators:	5	4	3	2	1
People favoring off-road vehicle use, through					
communicating with agency personnel:	5	4	3	2	1
administrative or court challenges:	5	4	3	2	1
pressure on legislators:	5	4	3	2	1
People favoring wilderness/preservation, through					
communicating with agency personnel:	5	4	3	2	1
administrative or court challenges:	5	4	3	2	1
pressure on legislators:	5	4	3	2	1
Other: _____	5	4	3	2	1

Participants received five copies of Part 2 (blank contact forms). Only one is included here.

PART 2: KEY CONTACTS

Please indicate, to the best of your recollection, the following information about those people outside the agency whom you consider to be key contacts. (Please include as many people as you consider to be key contacts. If additional space is needed, feel free to write on back of this form.):

Example

1. Name of Individual:	*Bill Smith*
2. Phone/Address (if available):	*(614) 555-1234; PO Box 100, Athens, OH 45700*
3. Group Affiliation (if any):	*Audubon Society, Athens Chapter*
4. His/Her Main Forest Concerns:	*Riparian protection, less timber harvesting, no clearcuts*

5. Contact Type & Frequency: *I call him whenever an Environmental Assessment is completed, which is about once a month.*
I meet with him on the Athens Watershed Committee quarterly.
He phones me about specific issues once or twice a week; he writes a letter about once a month.

6. Usefulness of Input: *A lot of his phone calls involve details that are better handled by others, but the contacts are helpful in my understanding of where the environmentalists stand on certain decisions. His input often fails to consider the needs of the local forest community.*

---

1. Name of Individual:

2. Phone/Address (if available):

3. Group Affiliation (if any):

4. His/Her Main Forest Concerns:

5. Types and Frequency of Contacts:

6. Usefulness of Input:

---

1. Name of Individual:

2. Phone/Address (if available):

3. Group Affiliation (if any):

4. His/Her Main Forest Concerns:

5. Types and Frequency of Contacts:

6. Usefulness of Input:

Appendix B
Statistical Tests for State and Federal Differences

This appendix contains information about the statistical tests I conducted throughout the study. Data reported below are supplemental to data reported in the main body of this manuscript (chapters 4 and 8).

For the data in Table 8.1 I performed pooled t-tests by using Microsoft Excel 5.0 software. I calculated t-values and corresponding p-values with the assumption of equal variances between the two populations (state and federal officials). A one-tailed test is appropriate because the expectation is that, for each interest type, officials at one level of governance perceive greater influence from a particular interest type than do officials at the other level of governance. I completed additional calculations without the assumption of equal population variances, and the results were virtually identical to those obtained under the assumption of equal population variances.

For the data in Table 8.3 I aggregated responses to each of the fourteen questionnaire items into two categories by agency type (state and federal). For each agency within each questionnaire item, I examined the distribution of responses for normality. Responses to seven of the questionnaire items exhibited a normal distribution across both agency types. For these normally distributed responses, I performed pooled t-tests with Stata 3.1 software. I performed calculations of t-values and corresponding p-values with the assumption of equal variances between the two populations (state and federal officials). Statistical data are listed in Table B.1.

Table B.1. Mean Response Values from Officials' Questionnaires, Part I

	State Officials:			Federal Officials:			t-	p-
Item	Mean	SD	N	Mean	SD	N	value	value
Ecosys. focus	0.62	0.99	39	0.78	0.90	36	−0.74	0.461
Horse trails	0.13	1.01	39	0.26	1.01	35	−0.55	0.584
Hiking trails	0.56	0.85	39	0.97	0.75	35	−2.18	0.033[a]
Oil/gas/min.	−0.51	0.89	39	−0.43	0.82	35	−0.42	0.673
Timber	0.44	1.02	39	0.17	0.85	36	1.24	0.220
Hunt/fish	0.58	0.78	40	0.60	0.70	35	−0.15	0.885
Local econ.	0.53	0.79	40	0.50	0.70	36	0.15	0.884

[a]Significant at 0.05 level.

I performed additional calculations without the assumption of equal population variances, and the results were virtually identical to those obtained under the assumption of equal population variances.

Responses for the remaining seven questionnaire items were not normally distributed. Clearly, responses to these items were not most frequently in the middle of the −2 to 2 scale. For example, officials across both agencies consistently valued increasing ORV trails at −2 or −1. For these nonparametric distributions, the pooled t-test is not an appropriate technique. Instead, a nonparametric test such as the Kolmogorov-Smirnov (K-S) test is needed. The K-S test involves measuring the maximum difference, D, between the

Table B.2. Mean Response Values from Officials' Questionnaires, Part II

	State Officials:			Federal Officials:				p-
Item	Mean	SD	N	Mean	SD	N	D	value
Rec. use fees	0.60	0.90	40	1.20	0.72	35	0.243	0.159
Public input	0.90	0.93	40	1.11	0.85	36	0.131	0.858
Camping	−0.21	0.95	39	0.31	1.05	35	0.261	0.112
ORV trails	−0.77	1.09	39	−0.56	1.11	36	0.094	0.993
Native sp.	0.71	0.90	38	0.94	0.89	36	0.146	0.759
Wild/preserv.	0.03	1.27	39	0.36	0.99	36	0.190	0.417
Clearcutting	1.48	0.60	40	0.42	1.30	36	0.506	0.000[a]

[a]Significant at 0.01 level.

Table B.3. Officials' Length of Employment with Agency

Agency	N	Mean Length of Employment (years)	SD	Pooled t-test:	
				t-value	p-value
Federal	42	18.6	7.47		
State	44	13.8	6.87		
Combined	86			−3.08	0.0028

cumulative frequency distributions of the two samples (Blalock 1972: 262). The maximum difference is used to calculate a p-value for each sample and for the samples combined. Results from Stata 3.1, presented in Table B.2, show a p-value of less than 0.05 for only one questionnaire item.

For the data in Table 8.4 I conducted pooled t-tests with Stata 3.1. I calculated t-values and corresponding p-values with the assumption of equal variances between the two populations (state and federal officials). The values are listed in Table B.3.

I conducted additional calculations without the assumption of equal population variances, and the results were virtually identical to those obtained under the assumption of equal population variances.

For the data in Table 8.5 I measured mobility as the average number of years per location that an official spent within the organization. For federal officials, the organization was the USDA Forest Service; state officials' organizations were the state forest agencies. I performed pooled t-tests with Stata 3.1. I calculated t-values and corresponding p-values with the assumption of equal variances between the two populations (state and federal officials). The values are given in Table B.4.

I conducted additional calculations without the assumption of equal population variances, and the results were virtually identical to those obtained under the assumption of equal population variances.

Table B.4. Officials' Geographic Mobility within Organization

Agency	N	Mean No. of Years per Location	SD	Pooled t-test:	
				t-value	p-value
Federal	42	5.1	3.02		
State	44	7.3	3.52		
Combined	86			2.99	0.0037

References

Anton, Thomas. 1989. *American Federalism and Public Policy*. New York: Random House.

Arnold, Douglas. 1979. *Congress and the Bureaucracy: A Theory of Influence*. New Haven, Conn.: Yale University Press.

Arnstein, Sherry R. 1969. "A Ladder of Citizen Participation." *American Institute of Planners Journal* 35:216–24.

Baden, John, and Richard Stroup, eds. 1981. *Bureaucracy vs. Environment: The Environmental Costs of Bureaucratic Governance*. Ann Arbor: University of Michigan Press.

Barney, Daniel. 1974. *The Last Stand*. New York: Grossman.

Bendor, Jonathan. 1990. "Formal Models of Bureaucracy: A Review." In *Public Administration: The State of the Discipline*, edited by Aaron Wildavsky and Naomi Lynn. Chatham, N.J.: Chatham House.

Bendor, Jonathan, Serge Taylor, and Roland Van Gaalen. 1987. "Stacking the Deck: Bureaucratic Missions and Policy Design." *American Political Science Review* 81:873–96.

Blalock, Hubert, Jr., 1972. *Social Statistics*. New York: McGraw-Hill.

Bowman, Ann, and Richard Kearney. 1986. *The Resurgence of the States*. Englewood Cliffs, N.J.: Prentice-Hall.

Brown, Greg, and Charles Harris. 2000. "The U.S. Forest Service: Whither the New Resource Management Paradigm?" *Journal of Environmental Management* 58:1–19.

Brune, Tom. 1996. "Washington's War of the Owls Heads toward a Compromise." *Christian Science Monitor*, 19 November, 3.

Budiansky, Stephen. 1991. "Sawdust and Mirrors: The Forest Service's Unusual Bookkeeping Is Costing the Environment and the Public Plenty." *U.S. News and World Report*, 1 July, 55–57.

Cigler, B. 1993. "Professionalizing the American States in the 1990s." *International Journal of Public Administration* 16(12):1965–2000.

Clarke, Jeanne N., and Daniel McCool. 1985. *Staking Out the Terrain: Power Differentials among Natural Resource Management Agencies*. Albany: State University of New York Press.

Cramer, Lori, James Kennedy, Richard Krannich, and Thomas Quigley. 1993. "Changing Forest Service Values and Their Implications for Land Management Decisions Affecting Resource-Dependent Communities." *Rural Sociology* 58(3):475–91.

Cubbage, Frederick, Jay O'Laughlin, and Charles Bullock III. 1993. *Forest Resource Policy*. New York: John Wiley and Sons.

Davis, David. 1993. *Energy Politics*. New York: St. Martin's Press.

Derthick, Martha. 1971. *The Influence of Federal Grants*. Cambridge, Mass.: Harvard University Press.

DiIulio, John D., Jr. 1994. "Principled Agents: The Cultural Bases of Behavior in a Federal Government Bureaucracy." *Journal of Public Administration Research and Theory* 4(3):277–318.

Downs, Anthony. 1957. *An Economic Theory of Democracy*. New York: Harper & Row.

Eisinger, Peter. 1988. *The Rise of the Entrepreneurial State: State and Local Economic Development Policy in the United States*. Madison: University of Wisconsin Press.

Eisner, Marc Allen, and Kenneth Meier. 1990. "Presidential Control versus Bureaucratic Power: Explaining the Reagan Revolution in Antitrust." *American Journal of Political Science* 34:269–87.

Franklin, Jerry. 1993. "The Fundamentals of Ecosystem Management with Applications in the Pacific Northwest." In *Defining Sustainable Forestry*, edited by Gregory Aplet, Nels Johnson, and Jeffrey T. Olson Unk. Washington, D.C.: Island Press.

Gibbins, Roger. 1994. "The Challenge of New Politics and New Social Movements to the Future of Federalism." In *Federalism and the New World Order*, edited by Stephen Randall and Roger Gibbins. Calgary, Canada: University of Calgary Press.

Gilless, Keith, Robert Lee, Bruce Lippke, and Paul Sommers. 1990. "Three-State Impact of Spotted Owl Conservation and Other Timber Harvest Reductions: A Comparative Evaluation of the Economic and Social Impacts." Seattle: Institute of Forest Resources, College of Forest Resources, University of Washington. September (#69).

Goetz, Edward. 1995. "Potential Effects of Federal Policy Devolution on Local Housing Expenditures." *Publius* 25(3):99–117.

Greer, Edward. 1979. *Big Steel*. New York: Monthly Review Press.

Halperin, Morton. 1974. *Bureaucratic Politics and Foreign Policy*. Washington, D.C.: Brookings Institution Press.

Heclo, Hugh. 1978. "Issue Networks and the Executive Establishment." In *The New American Political System*, edited by Anthony King. Washington, D.C.: American Enterprise Institute for Public Policy Research.

Hendee, John, and Randall Pitstick. 1994. "Growth and Change in U.S. Forest-Related Environmental Groups." *Journal of Forestry* 92(6):24–31.

Hoberg, George. 1992. *Pluralism by Design: Environmental Policy and the American Regulatory State*. New York: Praeger.

———. 1997. "From Localism to Legalism: The Transformation of Federal Forest Policy." In *Western Public Lands and Environmental Politics*, edited by Charles Davis. Boulder, Colo.: Westview Press.

Idaho Statesman. 1998. "Land Board Urged to Seek OK for Program; Experiment Would Let States, Groups Help Manage Forests." 22 July.

Kaufman, Herbert. 1960. *The Forest Ranger*. Baltimore: Resources for the Future.

Kelly, David, and Gary Braasch. 1988. *Secrets of the Old Growth Forest*. Salt Lake City, Utah: Peregrine Smith Books.

Kritz, Margaret. 1989. "Ahead of the Feds." *National Journal*, 9 December, 2989–93.

Krutilla, John, and John Haigh. 1978. "An Integrated Approach to National Forest Management." *Environmental Law* 8:373–415.

Larson, Erik. 1995. "Unrest in the West." *Time* 146 (23 October), 52.

Leal, Donald. 1995. "Turning a Profit on Public Forests." PERC Policy Series PS-4. Bozeman, Mont.: Political Economy Research Center.

Lee, Kai. 1993. *Compass and Gyroscope: Integrating Science and Politics for the Environment*. Washington, D.C.: Island Press.

Leopold, Aldo. 1949. *A Sand County Almanac*. New York: Oxford University Press.

Lowe, George, and Thomas Pinhey. 1982. "Rural-Urban Differences in Support for Environmental Protection." *Rural Sociology* 47(1):114–28.

Lowry, William. 1992. *The Dimensions of Federalism: State Governments and Pollution Control Policies*. Durham, N.C.: Duke University Press.

Margolis, Jon. 1997. "This Year, Congress Slunk into Washington." *High Country News* 29(1), 27 January, 5.

Marshall, Catherine, and Gretchen Rossman. 1989. *Designing Qualitative Research*. Newbury Park, Calif.: Sage Publications.

Maxey, William. 1996. "Foresters: Another Endangered Species?" *Journal of Forestry* 94(8):44.

Meier, Kenneth J. 1993. *Politics and the Bureaucracy: Policymaking in the Fourth Branch of Government*. Monterey, Calif.: Brooks/Cole Publishing.

Moe, Terry. 1989. "The Politics of Bureaucratic Structure." In *Can the Government Govern?* edited by John Chubb and Paul Peterson. Washington, D.C.: Brookings Institution Press.

Nash, Roderick. 1982. *Wilderness and the American Mind.* New Haven, Conn.: Yale University Press.

Nelson, Marj. 1999. "Habitat Conservation Planning." *Endangered Species Bulletin* 24(6):12–13.

Nelson, Robert, ed. 1995. *Public Lands and Private Rights: The Failure of Scientific Management.* Lanham, Md.: Rowman and Littlefield.

Niskanen, William. 1971. *Bureaucracy and Representative Government.* Chicago: Aldine-Atherton.

Oates, Wallace. 1991. *Studies in Fiscal Federalism.* Brookfield, Vt.: E. Elgar.

Ohio Department of Natural Resources. 1993. "Ohio's State Forests."

Ohio Division of Forestry. 1995. "State Forest Procedures Manual."

Oregon Department of Forestry. 1995. "Thanks for Asking about State Forest Lands."

Orren, Karen. 1974. *Corporate Power and Social Change.* Baltimore: Johns Hopkins University Press.

Ostrom, Elinor. 1990. *Governing the Commons: The Evolution of Institutions for Collective Action.* Cambridge, England: Cambridge University Press.

Ostrom, Elinor, Roy Gardner, and James Walker. 1994. *Rules, Games, and Common-Pool Resources.* Ann Arbor: University of Michigan Press.

Ostrom, Vincent. 1987. *The Political Theory of a Compound Republic: Designing the American Experiment.* San Francisco: ICS Press.

Ostrom, Vincent, Charles Tiebout, and Robert Warren. 1961. "The Organization of Government in Metropolitan Areas: A Theoretical Inquiry." *American Political Science Review* 55:831–42.

O'Toole, Randal. 1988. *Reforming the Forest Service.* Washington, D.C.: Island Press.

———. 1993. "Last Stand: Selling Out the National Forests." *Multinational Monitor* (January/February), 25–29.

Ott, J. Steven. 1989. *Organizational Cultural Perspective.* Pacific Grove, Calif.: Brooks/Cole.

Parker, Glenn. 1989. *Characteristics of Congress: Patterns in Congressional Behavior.* Englewood Cliffs, N.J.: Prentice-Hall.

Peterson, Paul. 1981. *City Limits.* Chicago: University of Chicago Press.

———. 1995. *The Price of Federalism.* Washington, D.C.: Brookings Institution Press.

Peterson, Paul, Barry Rabe, and Kenneth Wong. 1986. *When Federalism Works.* Washington, D.C.: Brookings Institution Press.

Pinchot, Gifford. 1947. *Breaking New Ground.* New York: Harcourt, Brace, and Co.

Pressman, Jeffrey, and Aaron Wildavsky. 1984. *Implementation,* 3d ed. Berkeley: University of California Press.

Rabe, Barry. 1986. *Fragmentation and Integration in State Environmental Management.* Washington, D.C.: Conservation Foundation.

Rauber, Paul. 1995. "National Yard Sale." *Sierra* 80(5):28.

Register-Guard [Eugene, Ore.]. 1996. "Applying the O&C Breaks." 25 July.

Rice, Richard. 1989. *National Forests: Policies for the Future,* vol. 5. Washington, D.C.: Wilderness Society.

Rich, Robert, and William White. 1996. "Health Care Policy and the American States: Issues of Federalism." In *Health Policy, Federalism, and the American States,* edited by Robert Rich and William White. Washington, D.C.: Urban Institute Press.

Ringquist, Evan. 1990. *Regulating Air and Water Quality: Politics and Progress at the State Level.* Ann Arbor, Mich.: UMI Dissertation Services.

Robinson, Glen. 1975. *The Forest Service.* Baltimore: Johns Hopkins University Press.

Ross, Stephen A. 1973. "The Economic Theory of Agency: The Principal's Problem." *American Economic Review* 12:134–39.

Roush, G. Jon. 1989. "The Disintegrating Web: The Causes and Consequences of Extinction." *Nature Conservancy Magazine* (November/December): 4–15.

Sabatier, Paul. 1974. "State and Local Environmental Policy: A Modest Review of Past Efforts and Future Topics." In *Environmental Politics,* edited by Stuart Nagel. New York: Praeger.

Sabatier, Paul, John Loomis, Catherine McCarthy. 1995. "Hierarchical Controls, Professional Norms, Local Constituencies, and Budget Maximization: An Analysis of U.S. Forest Service Planning Decisions." *American Journal of Political Science* 39(1):204–42.

Satchell, Michael. 1996. "At War in an Ancient Forest." *U.S. News and World Report,* 23 September, 74–76.

Schattschneider, E. 1960. *The Semisovereign People: A Realist's View of Democracy in America.* New York: Holt, Rinehart, and Winston.

Schlozman, K., and J. Tierney. 1983. "More of the Same: Washington Pressure Group Activity in a Decade of Change." *Journal of Politics* 45:351–75.

Scholz, John. 1988. "Federal Versus State Enforcement: Does It Matter?" In *Power Divided: Essays on the Theory and Practice of Federalism,* edited by Harry N. Scheiber and Malcolm M. Feeley. Berkeley: University of California Institute of Governmental Studies.

Shafritz, Jay, and E. W. Russell. 1997. *Introducing Public Administration.* New York: Longman.

Shepherd, Jack. 1975. *The Forest Killers*. New York: Weybright and Talley.

Shindler, Bruce, Brent Steel, and Peter List. 1996. "Public Judgments of Adaptive Management." *Journal of Forestry* 94(6):4–12.

Souder, Jon A., and Sally K. Fairfax. 1996. *State Trust Lands: History, Management, and Sustainable Use*. Lawrence: University Press of Kansas.

Spurr, Stephen, and Burton Barnes. 1980. *Forest Ecology*. New York: John Wiley and Sons.

Stuebner, Stephen. 2001. "Idaho Reaches for Control of the ESA." *High Country News*, 21 May. Available at www.hcn.org/servlets/hcn.Article?article_id=10520 (accessed February 11, 2001).

Swartz, Thomas, and John Peck, eds. 1990. *The Changing Face of Fiscal Federalism*. Armonk, N.Y.: M. E. Sharpe.

Thompson, Frank, and Michael Scicchitano. 1985. "State Enforcement of Federal Regulatory Policy: The Lessons of OSHA." *Policy Studies Journal* 13(3):591–98.

Tiebout, Charles. 1956. "A Pure Theory of Local Expenditures." *Journal of Political Economy* 64(5):416–24.

Tipple, Terence, and J. Douglas Wellman. 1991. "Herbert Kaufman's Forest Ranger Thirty Years Later: From Simplicity and Homogeneity to Complexity and Diversity." *Public Administration Review* 51(5):421–28.

Tremblay, K. R., Jr., and R. E. Dunlap. 1978. "Rural-Urban Residence and Concern with Environmental Quality: A Replication." *Rural Sociology* 43(3):474–91.

Twight, B. W., and F. J. Lyden. 1988. "Multiple Use vs. Organizational Commitment." *Forest Science* 34:474–86.

U.S. Department of Agriculture (USDA) Forest Service. 1964. "A History of the Siuslaw National Forest."

———. 1990. *Indiana's Timber Resource*. North Central Forest Experiment Station, St. Paul, Minn.

———. 1993a. *Forest Statistics for Ohio*. Northeastern Forest Experiment Station, Radnor, Pa.

———. 1993b. *A Draft Glossary for Ecosystem Management*. Pacific Northwest Region, Portland, Ore.

———. 1993c. *Forest Resources of the United States: General Technical Report RM-234*. Washington, D.C.

U.S. Department of Commerce. 1995a. *Regional Economic Information System* (CD-ROM). Economics and Statistics Administration, Bureau of Economic Analysis, Regional Economic Measurement Division. Washington, D.C. May.

————. 1995b. *1992 Census of Manufactures, Industry Series, Logging Camps, Sawmills, and Planing Mills.* Economic and Statistics Administration, Bureau of the Census. Washington, D.C.

U.S. General Accounting Office (GAO). 1999. "Recreation Fees: Demonstration Program Successful in Raising Revenues but Could Be Improved." GAO/T-RCED-99-77.

Vig, Norman, and Michael Kraft, eds. 2000. *Environmental Policy: New Directions for the Twenty-first Century.* 4th ed. Washington, D.C.: CQ Press.

Walker, J. 1983. "The Origins and Maintenance of Interest Groups in America." *American Political Science Review* 77:390–406.

Warrick, Joby. 1997. "U.S. Lost $15 Million Selling Public Timber." *Washington Post,* 21 November, A25.

Washington State Department of Natural Resources. 1994. "Map of Washington State Major Public Lands." Olympia, Wash.

Wayne National Forest. 1996. "History—Wayne N.F." April.

Weber, Max. 1968 [1947]. *The Theory of Social and Economic Organization.* New York: Oxford University Press.

White, Leonard. 1953. *The States and the Nation.* Baton Rouge: Louisiana State University Press.

Yozwiak, Steve. 1996. "Ranchers Face Lawsuit: U.S. Official Claims Abuse." *Arizona Republic,* 4 June, A1.

Ziegler, L. Harmon, and Hendrik van Dahlen. 1976. "Interest Groups in State Politics." In *Politics in the American States, A Comparative Analysis,* edited by Herbert Jacob and Kenneth Vines. Boston: Little, Brown.

Index

Note: Page references followed by "t" or "f" indicate tables and figures.